GW00771437

Universal Lessons from a

Global Traveller

39 Key Road-Signs To Help Navigate Your Career

By

John Mainwaring

Table of Contents

Dedication i

Acknowledgements ii

About the Author iii

Do Not Be Afraid To Promote Yourself............................1

Temper Your Ambition To Succeed 3

Establishing a Rapport with Customers and Suppliers. 4

Contracts 7

Delegation 9

Position Trading 12

Ways to Determine Strength in a Market.........................15

Developing a New Market 16

Claims / Debt 17

Communication 21

Do Not Guarantee the "Arrival" of Material....................23

Increase in Customs Duties – An Opportunity?...............24

Rights and Wrongs...25

Rule of Law..26

Respect for a Country's Customs......................................27

If You Made a Mistake, Front It Up. Admit It.................29

Honesty with Customers 30

Don't Lie 31

Speeches...32

Think – Write – Rethink – Transmit................................33

You Are Not an Island 34

Can You Help Me? 35

Food 36

How to Handle Staff When You Are the "New Kid on the Block" 37

Where Taking Action Against an Employee May Bring You into Conflict with the Law 41

Interviewing 42

Impressions 44

Receiving the Benefit Of The Doubt 45

Travel – If You Have The Opportunity… Grab It 46

Be the Best 47

Culture Shock… and Reverse Culture Shock! 49

Coping with a Negative Frame of Mind 51

Be Yourself 54

Do Not Be Embarrassed by Your Lack of Knowledge 55

Between a Rock and a Hard Place 56

Loss of Employment / Redundancy 58

Don't Discount Experience 64

My Creed / Sense of Humour 65

Last Word…Appreciation of Age…at My Age 66

Dedication

This book is dedicated to my wife – Betsy, who has not only been with me in the good times but has been a tower of strength to me in those challenging moments life throws up at you.

Acknowledgements

I wish to acknowledge the immeasurable help given to me by Betsy, my wife, Virginia, my daughter, her husband, Jez, my brother-in-law Dr Tim Bralower and Kieron Launder in compiling this record of my life-experiences.

Their inspiration and initiatives have been invaluable. I am deeply indebted to them.

About the Author

It is said that everyone "has a book in him". I'm about to find out!

I visit a coffee shop most Saturdays and remain perplexed, though less so as time passes, that the British economy can survive, if not thrive, without me. Why are my services and my experience not being called upon? My degree of perplexity diminishes as I accept that the world can indeed survive without me. The man in his late thirties opposite me, bouncing his child upon his lap, no doubt has a well-paid job. His wife looks secure that hubby is working whilst she accepts enforced premature retirement to look after the wealth creators of tomorrow.

How presumptuous can I be? Well, why not? Why can't I believe that I still have a contribution to make? If I don't have such self-belief, two things can happen. First, I can roll over and play dead in the belief that no one wants to hear from me, and second, this prophesy becomes self-fulfilling. What a waste. But if you do not believe in yourself, how can you expect others to do so? It is a quirk of human nature that to prove one's worth and secure some fulfilment from one's life, one must have confidence in one's self. But how to gain it? Character? Education? Parental Up-Bringing? Perhaps all three and more. Follow one's instincts. Place inhibitions to one side. Give it a go.

This leads to the next predicament, what exactly should you do to show your self-worth? How do you secure that fulfilment in your life?

I thought the answer was in a hope and a prayer that, somehow, I would be called back to my office. "John. We have missed you. Where have you been?" But things move on. Not only in the way business is conducted but the personalities involved. You can return as the wise old man, but the personalities change. Sure, due respect will be afforded to you, but you are not the generation for the future. The customer sitting across the table is not the person you knew but his son or daughter. They will want to make their own mark on the business, as did their father. Most probably, you will not be seen as a person to realise their vision. So, your place has limited utility.

What then?

Re-invent yourself. Do not look to Christmas-past. Do not try to relive the "old days", as they really will not be the same. Do something which will enable others to inherit. Provide a legacy. Not for money necessarily; you probably already have that in hand, but a legacy by which you will be remembered in the affections of others.

It has to be different from whatever you have done in the past, and it has to be fulfilling. It has to give you self-worth. Paint a picture. Write a book!!!

Having been made redundant in 2014 and thence self-propelled into a joint venture with ex-colleagues whose DNA was not a match for mine, the time to "hang up my boots" was indeed premature. So, for the last three years, I have been trying to find substitutes for the cut and thrust of the trading world.

To date, my time has been spent predominantly playing golf and bridge. The former has maintained my sanity; the latter has exacted its toll on my intellect! None has proven to be a satisfying substitute for "trading", thus it was at breakfast in Raleigh Durham when I was asked by my brother in law's son what commercial lessons can I offer that my verbose replies prompted me to produce a compendium which is in part autobiographical and in part a reflection of my life-experiences/lessons in business over the last 47+ years, hopefully with a smattering of humour to maintain your interest.

This Ladies and Gentlemen, is my starting point, a legacy. A synopsis, in part, of my life, or parts of it, which I leave to my children and grandchildren. For posterity.

To reflect on the above, I have devoted approximately the first one-third of this book to my autobiography. I want you to read this first section not only because you may find it entertaining but because it may make you aware that the world is there to explore. It is there for you to take. Accept the challenge. Sure, you can pursue extremely worthwhile careers in the UK. Of course, that is so true, but to travel is to push those boundaries, not just the physical boundaries but the metaphysical boundaries.

What do you do when a challenge confronts you? A challenge, by its very definition, evokes feelings of uncertainty. Do you "take it on", confront it, or do you steer clear? Let me, in turn, be clear, I am not inciting the abandonment of the rationale, but I want you to assess a challenge where risk is not totally eradicated. How refreshing is that?!

The answer to the above question, by the way, is not straightforward, but one thought for you to cogitate upon is this, better to take the risk and regret it rather than regret taking the risk.

The second part of this book relates to life lessons. These are drawn from my own personal experiences in trading metals. Not all the life lessons I have described will be relevant to you, but for sure, there will be some, hopefully many, which will resonate with you.

I want you to read the second part of this book because:

a) It will teach you how to handle many real-life situations which are thrust upon you either by design or by chance. Situations that you are compelled to face and resolve.

b) It will make you aware that even in today's world of advanced software, in the business environment in which we live, there is still a need for emotional intelligence, the need to communicate and rationalize human reasoning.

c) It espouses a set of sound values by which you are judged and by which others can be appraised.

So, before I delve into life lessons, let me give you some autobiographical details.

I went to Prep School in Wilmslow, Cheshire, where we lived at the time. I boarded at the same school when my father, who worked for Unilever, was posted down to London.

My Prep school left a substantial impression on me. It was here that both my conscious and unconscious biases evolved.

I believe there is a direct correlation between one's liking of a subject and your respect for the teacher who taught the subject.

For me, I loved History and English, which happened to be taught by the same person who happened to be my "favourite" teacher....John Kingdon.

It was John Kingdon who introduced me to the world of Boudica and the Iceni… of monks and monasteries… Fountains Abbey. He kindled my fascination in history from the Romans upto the Tudors via Thomas a Becket and Wat Tyler.

John Kingdon introduced me to classical music, Tchaikovsky's 1st piano concerto. Such music transports you into an orbit of cosmic vibration. Such music alone finds a resonance in the inner depths of your mind, and itself alone dictates when to lie in abeyance and when to visit the contemplative foremost of your thoughts.

To the candour of Carl Orff's Carmina Burana.

John Kingdon's home was in the Lake District. It was he who introduced me to the mountains. Being based in Wilmslow, we were but one and a half hours from The Lakes. There was a point in time when you could show me a photograph of anywhere in The Lakes, and I could give you its location.

Other teachers were memorable for different reasons. I received my first beating at my Prep school. It was for bad Latin. I can remember the Friday afternoon quite clearly… when everyone was preparing for the school Garden Party, I was confined to a classroom awaiting the Latin master and his cane. Shaking hands with him after the punishment was part of the ritual. Such was the dispensation of discipline in the 1960s!

As I gingerly sat in the classroom after receiving my beating, my thoughts were not for myself, not so contemplative. I was more concerned about how my father would react to the news. I remember walking back home and seeing my father pruning some roses. I told him of the events of the afternoon, to which he replied, "about time too". The events of that afternoon were crazy, but I ended up feeling strangely relieved!!

From Wilmslow, I passed Common Entrance to King's Canterbury. I was forever proud to have been educated in such an establishment. How lucky I was to have received such an education.

King's also gave me confidence which is still with me even today.

I was determined that my children should also benefit first-hand from such an education when their time came.

Before I entered King's, I went on a fact-finding mission with my parents to Canterbury principally to see another school there, not King's. In fact, it was only by chance, when walking through Canterbury, that we came across King's. I clearly remember asking my parents what were these impressive buildings in the precincts of the cathedral? I was advised it was King's.

Back at school in Wilmslow, I asked which was the better school. I was advised….King's. So I queried why I wasn't trying to gain a place at King's. This question seemed to resonate with my parents, who had made similar inquiries. From then on, we were of a single mind that I was to be educated at King's. It was a strange sequence of events. My striving for the best was really a result of being pushed principally by my mother. She always told me to "aim high".

From King's, I went straight to Kingston Polytechnic, now Kingston University.

I remember broaching my father about a "gap year". My well-rehearsed cadence was totally annihilated, vanquished. A rout of unfathomable proportions. Pleas-in-mitigation shredded. The earth continued on its rotation.

Having secured a Law Degree (2:2) at Kingston Polytechnic, my aspirations for a career in law awaited me.

I chose the path to practice as a Solicitor. The dedication the course demanded challenged my very commitment to follow in the steps of Perry Mason. It was at this time that I met my first wife. Actually, she is still my wife, Betsy, with whom we have two children, James and Virginia.

Let me digress for one paragraph about my family. Betsy has shown such guts and selfless determination in coping with the harder aspects of expatriate life. She is a tower of strength. James is currently in Berlin, running his own business designing and manufacturing furniture. It has been tough, but boy, has he shown tenacity and is now reaping the rewards of his past sacrifices. Virginia is successfully climbing the corporate ladder and has a senior position in a U.S. rating agency, and is married to Jez, an accomplished entrepreneur. They have two mini-terrorists, Bella and Max, for whom we baby-sit every Friday.

Romance certainly steered me off course! I did not pass my Part 2 exams, much to the chagrin of my parents, and whilst my failure here opened up a vista of unfathomable opportunity, further academic study was not a path I wished to consider.

Six months on a building site gave me a chance to secure some funds yet also the chance to delve into the pages of The Times to find what global enticements awaited me.

I ventured into the world of metals trading.

My career opened tremendous opportunities for me. I counted that I have visited and concluded business in a total of 69 countries. I just loved to travel and still do. Travel broadens your horizons. New experiences. New cultures. Different values. You can drown yourself in all three and come out richer, and it will show. Your education never ends. Travel is a huge part of it.

Experiences, be they good or bad, are always memorable, and human nature is such that you will always put on a humorous or brave face even when recollecting the most dire of circumstances.

Of the 69 countries I visited, there were seven countries where we lived for a prolonged period of 3-6 years, namely: Trinidad, Sudan, India, Belgium, Switzerland, Singapore, and Dubai.

My first posting was to Trinidad at the age of 23. In this post, I covered most of the Caribbean and various countries in South America.

One such country was Guyana which I visited every month.

The 07.00 flight from Georgetown, Guyana, back to Port of Spain, Trinidad, necessitated a taxi ride commencing at around 4.30 am. The ride would take approximately one hour.

MOT tests were not de rigour in Guyana, so you can guess that the average taxi had little safety features.

The trip to the airport passes through uninhabited remote forestation, not the place to discover one has a puncture.

The driver, who had clearly been auditioning but rejected by McLaren's F1 team, pulled out the jack and proceeded to loosen the nuts on the culprit wheel.

With a new inflated wheel in place, we had one problem. We could not find the nuts in the darkness. The new moon offered its face, but the shadow of the forest smothered its radiance, so both driver and passengers proceeded to grovel on the ground feeling for the nuts. Ten minutes of close inspection of the undergrowth rendered no result, whereupon the driver proceeded to take one nut off the other three wheels and affix them to the wheel in question. One Hillman Hunter thence disappeared down the road with four inflated wheels, three nuts on each wheel. The fact that the car had a certain sideways gyration was of little consequence.

Trinidad itself presented its own challenges. One's own personal safety was ever-present in your mind. All houses had grills over their downstairs windows, and it was not unusual to have a gate at the bottom of your stairs which you would lock to give you some peace of mind in the hours of slumber.

Like any tropical island, Trinidad had two seasons, wet and dry. Think of the wet season, and one-word springs to mind, drainage.

Rain in Trinidad was unconstrained and totally disobliging. It did not respect ordained channels for its disbursement.

Invariably it would choose the telephone network to wreak havoc on the population. This resulted in even more sporadic communication and ever-more aggravation. I do not think it was my imagination when I thought I heard gurgling sounds down the phone. I did wonder, though, if my customers had submerged themselves in an amphibious attempt to take my call.

Hiring staff in Trinidad was yet another challenge. It was a source of consternation to a prospective secretary that to make a telephone call, lifting the receiver off the telephone apparatus was obligatory.

The same lady would wrestle with the notion of error-free typing. In those days, manual type-writers were used, not computers. Type-writers used paper. Shall we say she challenged the global availability of such parchment?

After spending three years in Trinidad, I was offered a posting in East Africa covering Sudan and Kenya. I thought, Nairobi, why not? It was a civilized place. However, my dreams were redirected toward reality when I was advised that I would have to be based in Khartoum! The reasoning behind this was that the Company had greater problems in Sudan than in Kenya, with the allocation of foreign exchange being a primary factor.

Mention that you are being posted to Sudan, and immediately you hear an echo "Sudan"????!!!!!

Sudan was a tough place to live. I had married just six months earlier, so you can imagine the enticement to a new wife of the picture postcard beaches of the Caribbean or food shortages in a sand-swept bunker in East Africa.

Before I accepted the posting, I made certain investigations as to whether it really was appropriate to take a young wife there.

Betsy had a contact in Shell. The report she received was surprisingly favourable. What we didn't realize was that her contact was living in a most majestic colonial house on the banks of the Nile with its own pool and jetty. In contrast, we moved into a two-bedroom house with two borrowed beds, two borrowed chairs, and a thermos of cold water.

Through my wife's connections in the American community, we were able to purchase the most exquisite furniture from those completing their posting, so within one month, we had a well-furnished abode.

Our next problem was electricity. We endured power cuts every day, which was of little consequence in the daytime as we both worked. However, power cuts at night tested our sense of humour.

The heat, even at night, was so intense that we could not sleep inside, so I remember we endured eleven consecutive nights sitting outside on our veranda. My company was not very sympathetic to my plight to purchase a generator; after all, I had had a predecessor in Sudan who never made such a request. What the Company did not know was that he was a single person whose nocturnal pursuits did not encompass sleeping, at least not in *his* bed.

Whilst the attitude of my Company was uncompromising, our response upon reflection was perhaps a little mystifying. My thoughts were that if the company was not going to give me a generator, then I was determined to show them how invaluable I was to them. This guileless, naïve thought process certainly showed humility, if not a lack of self-confidence. How many people were lining up outside my M.D.'s office to hop on a plane to fly to Sudan to replace me? Not many…I would surmise! Even so, we persisted, and after three months, we became proud recipients of a generator.

A generator was to make an immeasurable improvement to our lives. However, first, we had to overcome the problem of where to find diesel fuel.

We were rationed to three gallons of petrol every three days. Diesel was even more elusive.

My company had a contract with the Sudanese Army to supply certain spare parts to their Land Rovers. This necessitated visits to their base, where the soldiers enjoyed a sumptuous breakfast of Nile perch and other indigenous specialities. On one occasion, the Colonel with whom I negotiated the spare parts asked if he could do anything for me. Within five minutes, I was driving a sergeant down to the depot where, upon his "nod", my car and the jerry cans I had in the back were filled to the brim with petrol. What a result!

With my supply problem of petrol largely resolved, this left the problem of re-supply of diesel to be resolved.

When one is an ex-patriot, the heads of other companies are more accessible to you. One's world is smaller. You meet them at cocktail parties or "Sudan Club" events. In this way, access to fuel is on tap. However, no one would want money for giving me diesel, that would be rather crude, pardon the pun, so I had to think of other inducements more palatable to them.

Beer.

Ancient Rome never had a god of beer, only wine, Bacchus.

Beer was extremely expensive in Sudan. This was not due to some budgetary exercise but more as a courtesy, a mark of respect, to Saudi Arabia, who gave Sudan copious amounts of dosh. So, through friends in a USA oil company, I was able to obtain unlimited supplies of canned beer. Thus I used to secure supplies of diesel by giving a case of beer to the heads of some of the foreign oil companies in Sudan in exchange for five gallons of diesel. True barter, except that I had to place a monetary value on the diesel in my colourful accounts presented monthly back to my London office.

We probably had more memorable experiences from our time in Sudan than from any of our other postings.

The Sudanese people were delightful with a true Bedouin temperament. Always ready to extend a hand of friendship and hospitality to you. This, from people who live in one of the poorest countries in Africa.

Khartoum, the capital, was at the centre of fierce fighting between the British and the Mahdi in the late 19th Century, circa 1898. After General Gordon was killed by the Mahdi in 1885 and revenge was exacted by Lord Kitchener at the Battle of Omdurman, Lord Kitchener left a permanent jingoistic mark on Khartoum by arranging all the roads in the centre of the city to form the shape of the Union Jack flag. Such imperialistic machinations exist today.

Irrespective of wealth, every country in the world appears to crave two things: an airline and a steel mill. Sudan was no exception.

Sudan Airways had recently acquired a Boeing 707 from Air Lingus. It was returning from a Haj run from Khartoum to Mecca when it hit a haboob (sand storm) and mistakenly took the lights of fishing boats in the Nile as the landing lights at Khartoum airport.

The plane crash landed into the Nile. Fortunately, there were no passengers, and all eleven of the crew escaped uninjured.

As an aside to this, the main mode of transport between villages in Sudan was by way of the truck, which would normally be embellished with hard wooden or metal benches for the passengers, be they humans, chickens, or goats!

Ten days after the above crash-landing, these trucks had refined their upholstery to "deluxe reclining seats". If you were really lucky, you also acquired a sick bag.

The truck owners had only just rowed out to the plane and stripped it of its seating!!

Perhaps the fishermen had also acquired a more relaxing pose for their nocturnal endeavours.

Whilst the indigenous people of Sudan were warm and accommodating, the reptiles which patrolled the majestic White and Blue Niles had other notions of hospitality.

Friday in Sudan was the one day in the week when one was not expected to work. Friends of ours had a house on the banks of the Blue Nile together with a grass tennis court, so post-siesta, we hot-footed it to this oasis of tranquillity.

We normally played three sets before fresh lemon quenched our thirst. On one occasion, however, a fifth participant appeared from between the sand dunes. His (well, it could have been a "her") impressive array of molars and incisors, coupled with a cavernous throat, brought our game to an abrupt end! The crocodile strode nonchalantly onto the court whilst we hastily arranged the appropriate barricade in the house! Eventually, this semi-aquatic reptile retreated to cooler climes. Regarding tennis, we called it a day. It was a snap decision.

Whilst Sudan was considered a "hardship" posting, my Director in London never quite appreciated the deprivations of the place….the sheer heat (up to 51 degrees C), the food shortages, the daily power cuts, and the fuel rationing (three gallons every three days) which severely curtailed one's social life. So, when the opportunity arose to give my Director a flavour of the daily challenges, I took it!!

The fuel shortages prevented us from taking the company car to visit all customers; thus, I would drive to his hotel, and thence we would take taxis thereafter.

One morning he appeared in a beautifully laundered light-blue shirt. Just the colour to reflect any possible unfortunate perspiration. Our schedule took us to Omdurman, which usually necessitated joining a traffic jam over the Omdurman Bridge.

The dastardly plan was to choose a taxi that had plastic as opposed to cloth seats. Taxi drivers happily drove up, thinking of the inflated fare they could charge hotel guests. One quick look inside the car to see cloth seats prompted me to dismiss them with a show of flailing arms and undecipherable Arabic. Eventually, one lucky driver with plastic seats meandered towards us.

Having joined the queue over the bridge, it took no more than five minutes for the heat to penetrate the car. The bespoke blue shirt was darkening in colour. We had a chameleon in the making. This, accompanied by the shuffling on the front seat and the wiping of the brow, hopefully, made my boss aware that Factor 50 did not contain all the answers to the African sun.

One knock-on effect of the power cuts in Sudan was the shortage of water. Another was the limited access to international phone lines.

To make any international call, one had to first phone the international operator. You were lucky if she gave you a "slot" on the same day. Invariably it was the next day. Of course, there were ways to secure a time of your choice. You just had to find them. Our contact had a penchant for Johnny Walker Black Label. She could afford the expensive taste!

The international written communication was by telex. Basically a glorified typing machine. Was there ever to be a variation in the flow of electricity to the machine, the message printed from the same would be garbled.

On one occasion, I received a telex from London requesting that I do not proceed on my two-week tour of Kenya, which I visited every six weeks.

It is perhaps hard to imagine how much we looked forward to these visits to Kenya. Sudan was our home, but living there was tough.

The reason London gave to me to delay my visit to Kenya was factually incorrect, though to be fair to London, they were not aware of the changed situation in Sudan, nor could I communicate the same to them. However, instead of appearing to over-rule London's decision, which would have brought a host of accusations of arrogance against me, the simplest solution was to re-type back to London "……telex garbled please repeat to Norfolk Hotel, Nairobi". Our sanity was saved!

With regard to water supplies in Sudan, water pumps provided the vital task of pushing the water from the mains into your tank. Well, that was the idea in principle.

On one occasion, I arrived back in Sudan from the U.K. to find that my water pump had burnt out. With no pump, I had no water in my house. Fortunately, a friend of mine was Head of Procurement at the US Embassy, so for USD 120.00, he could supply a water pump. In fact, it was a water pump designed to pump water up a four-storey apartment block.

I purchased the pump and arranged for local workmen to install it. However, instead of connecting the pipes in such a way as to pump water into my tank, they connected it so that it took the residue of water left in my tank out into the mains!

Despair turned to not-so-silent rage. Not only was I without water, but the existing pipes had been erroneously cut, and sawn, to accommodate this new 5-star pump. New pipes were in short supply, so we had no choice but to "re-extend" the pipes. This was only achieved by adding universal joint after universal joint until the original length of the pipe had been restored. It didn't look pretty, but my anger, my despair, and my thirst were all quenched.

Working in a scorched environment such as Khartoum certainly presented its own challenges.

My office in Khartoum was a perfectly adequate one-room at the top of our agent's building. Between me and the 51-degree searing heat outside was a false ceiling, stained by the residue of an infrequent rain storm, and some galvanized corrugated roofing, which my agents deemed had seen better days.

One morning I heard what I presumed were men clambering around the roof, ripping up the corrugated roofing.

I immediately called a halt to work as, being acutely aware of the scarcity of corrugated sheeting, I wanted some assurance that new sheeting was on hand to replace the sheets being removed.

My quick visit to the side of the building allayed my fears when I saw, for my own eyes, sparkling new sheets.

I was quite excited!

What I did not appreciate was that workmen were apparently more scarce than the materials they used. For the next ten days, no workmen appeared to replace the sheeting. So, with sun cream in hand, I spent the next week and a half in the office cabriolet style, under the direct glare of the sun with a sun hat and sun-screen, the only protection between me and the elements.

It was at this time that Khartoum experienced one of the many riots whipped up by the Muslim Brotherhood, an Islamist group founded in Egypt in the 1920s, which championed the rights of the poor or, frankly, any rights borne by the citizens of Sudan, which affronted its President.

Jaafar Nimeiry was the President of Sudan at that time. During the riots, his main concern was his ability to navigate between his palace and the polo fields. He had little time for those who pressed their flesh against his beige Rolls Royce in the pursuit of gruel or perhaps food of a less nutritious value, namely the flies which lay prostrate on his windscreen.

His well-rehearsed answer to such riots was the generous lobbying of tear gas canisters into the throng. On one occasion, the throng was outside my office on the ground, not on the roof. As for the reasons explained, I didn't have a roof. So, not only had I to contend with blistering heat, but I had to don a pair of goggles more appropriately found in a museum dedicated to the work of Jacques Cousteau.

My wife would arrive at my office via a circuitous route avoiding the tear gas and its effects. I had to explain to her that although I was pleased to see her, there were other reasons for the tears navigating the contours of my face.

From Sudan, my next tour took me to India, where I spent three years.

I loved the place. It is difficult to generalise, but Indians, to me, are an extremely intelligent and resourceful people.

India was a large part of the British Imperial crown, and some travellers foolishly think the same persists today, but Indians are very polite and very confident of their own capabilities, and justly so. They are also a respectful nation. They respect age and consider elders to be blessed with more wisdom. But, you would be a fool to take advantage of their respect.

The crowding and the dirt of a metropolis can "get to you". But, if one can place such experiences into context, countries like India are so rich in colour in life. It's a land of expectations, a land that will take those very expectations and turn them into fulfillment.

Indian businessmen generally started their formal day late, around 10.30 am, but ended their day equally late, around, say, 8.30 pm.

With London 5 1/2 hours behind in time, I was always keen to have my communications to London sitting on their desks upon their opening. 10.30 am starts did not help accommodate this, so I started seeing customers in their homes and invariably had breakfast with them. In fact, I saw a few customers more in their silk pyjamas than in their suits!

On one occasion, I was having breakfast with my customer whose father was choosing diamonds for his granddaughter's wedding.

Such opulence is rarely seen. When I attended the wedding, I saw a choker of diamonds, not a necklace, a choker!! As regards the earrings, well, I chased the bride around the room all afternoon, hoping one would fall off. I could then retire for life.

One last comment on India, which is an important point, is the appreciation of the Hindu caste system. I exclude from this the Parsis, the Zoroastrians who emigrated from Persia to India from the 8th century onwards to avoid persecution by the Arabs who overran the Persian Empire.

The Hindu caste system in India reflects one's own social standing in the community. There are four Hindu social classes, namely: Brahims, Kshatriyas, Vaishyas and Shrudas... in that order. I do not include the Dalits, the Untouchables

Within the above four social classes, there are approximately 3,000 castes and over 25,000 sub-castes.

The importance of one's identity within the above social classes/caste system really emanates from the decline of the Mughal era and the rise of the British Colonial Government.

An appreciation of the above social strata in India is to make you aware that:

1) It exists.
2) One perhaps needs to be at least sensitive to this structure when one is in a working environment and asking for members of different social classes to inter-react.

It's important.

With my delegate-ships abroad coming to an end, I continued my international travel using our head office in the UK as my base.

Iran was one such country I frequently visited, say approximately every six weeks.

The immigration arrangements for travel to Iran were such that you collected your visa in Tehran upon arrival, having already jumped through various hoops in the UK, including at Heathrow. Well, on one occasion, having satisfied the visa requirements at Heathrow, I arrived at 3 am into Tehran and went straight to the "Visa Desk". The official's diligent search for my visa was promptly halted when he discovered that I was British. "You have to leave", was his command. The recent dialogue between David Cameron, our Prime Minister, and the Ayatollah had not contributed to world peace. Business travellers like myself were to feel the brunt of this dialogue or lack of it!

I was escorted to a room that contained one chair. I was grateful it did not contain two; otherwise, interrogation may have been on the menu. Mind games started, hostage taking, etc. Room service was certainly a little slow. After three hours during which I learned various permutations of my twelve-digit Barclaycard number, the door swung open, and a swarthy gentleman, whose sense of humour was proving elusive, entered and motioned me to stand. His firm grip on my arm proved rather unromantic and detracted from the delights of seeing dawn appear over Tehran as I was escorted to the departure gate.

My escort released his grip once I had entered the plane, the same plane which brought me to Iran. So, I was being deported.

This was not my last visit to Iran, but it was my most memorable.

You don't go to places like Tehran without encountering some period in history. Countless times I would meet the British Ambassador in his magnificent residence. This was a residence that played a major part in the drafting and signing of the Treaty of Tehran in 1943. This was the treaty signed by Theodore Roosevelt, Stalin, and Churchill, which opened up a second front against Hitler, Operation Overlord, in World War Two.

My discussions with the Ambassador were in the same room where the Treaty of Tehran was, in part, negotiated between the big three Allied leaders. Being in that same room exposed one's soul and very being to the aggrandisement of that historic occasion.

My visits to Tehran always ended with a rushed visit to the Spice Shop. Here, I took out my shopping list impressed into my hand by my London office before leaving for the trip. Boxes of dates. Whatever you think dates do to your body, they are so succulent. The texture, the taste, and the moistness invited uninhibited indulgence. Saffron, the flower from the crocus, lay in abundance. The royalty of spices.

My memories of Iran do not permit me to forget my last visit to their passport control at the airport prior to departure. In front of me were three consanguineous gentlemen of non-Iranian descent dressed in full tribal splendour. Behind them and in front of me were three ladies also impressively dressed in full tribal regalia. Such dress hid both their identity and compass bearing. I invited them to proceed in front of me, whereupon they turned 180 degrees. The problem now facing me (or not facing me!!) was whether the ladies had turned to face me or turned away in disgust that a westerner would dare address them. What was happening three feet in front of me? Was I the witness to three voluptuous backsides pointing at me (for sure, the ladies were not calorie counting), or was I now facing three damsels about to exercise their right to peregrinate to fields afar?

They proceeded through passport control, and I proceeded after them.

My frequent visits to Iran were outnumbered only by my visits to Russia and Ukraine. In both Russia and Ukraine, the summers were hot, but the winters could be cold, bitterly cold. Cold, as in your tongue sticking to the roof of your mouth. On more than one occasion, I slept in my overcoat in my hotel room.

During my initial visits to Russia, I was able to tick off places that had been romanticised in my mind, The Kremlin, Red Square, The Bolschoi, St Petersburg, The Urals, Siberia.

In my youth, I was introduced to Tchaikovsky and Russian authors such as Dostoyevsky's "Crime and Punishment" Turgenev

"Fathers and Sons" and, of course, Tolstoy "Anna Karenina". I haven't a clue how my subconscious retained an affiliation here, but it did. So, here I was, able to visit places that had absorbed my adolescent curiosity.

The Urals appeared rather flat. It was here that Stalin brought his prisoners of war to help build vast industrial plants, many of which still survive today.

Russian prisoners and prisoners of war were the raw material used to promote Stalin's strategy of an industrial hinterland.

Russia, to me, always reflected England in the 19th Century, the very rich and the very poor. One of the reasons why the latter stayed poor was because they were never organized into any coherent body.

The wealth one witnessed appeared to know no bounds.

Every month I visited a steel mill in Siberia to secure an allocation of steel for the USA market. On one occasion, I was invited to visit a ski slope that the steel mill had carved out of the mountain for no other person than the President of Russia himself.

I had visions of being halfway up a ski lift and then being blessed with a power cut. How wrong was I? The ski lift and all the ensuing apparatus were top-of-the-range made in Austria. Pylons, gondolas, and switchboards, all made in Austria, and all for one man. Quite an indulgence.

Russia encapsulated a mood of self-help. The whole business environment encouraged a "take what you can for yourself" approach. Loyalty was only to yourself.

My experience in Ukraine pre-dates the current situation. There was no charismatic, principled figure running the country at that time. Indeed, Ukraine survived by a similar ethos to that espoused in Russia.

I used to spend two weeks every month travelling to the steel mills of Ukraine, trying to ascertain whether they could produce steel products to international specifications. Prior to Glasnost and Perestroika, the steel mills only produced to the Russian specification of "Gost." For Ukraine (and Russia, for that matter) to be able to sell on the international stage, their material had to comply with international specifications.

Prior to Perestroika, the steel mill received an order to produce a certain quantity and quality of steel. The steel was produced and thence transported from the mill by train. The mill had no idea where the steel was destined nor for what purpose.

Whilst the language barrier created a gulf in the communication between the officials working in the steel plants and me, no such barrier could hide the sheer joy and pride when we were able to confirm to these gentlemen and ladies that their steel met international specifications.

The amenities in Ukraine were extremely limited. In the early 1990s, there was only one restaurant in Kyiv serving western style food, and whilst I am "game" to try any international cuisine, the delicacies of Slavonic haute cuisine were beyond me. Thus many a time, I retired to my room with an element in hand to boil up pot noodles garnished with cream crackers.

Come the weekend, to pass the time, I would visit the opera house to witness the gracefulness of ballet and the emotion and passion of opera. In fact, the only place I have seen both art forms is in Russia and Ukraine. Regrettably, the lexical richness of the libretto eluded me.

The opulence of the Opera houses was the embodiment of a societal contradiction. Whatever one's views of Russia and Ukraine, we are all an intellectual hostage to the richness of their culture from the depth of their literature, their cathedrals built with lapis and malachite, to the vastness of their plains. What mind can be chained, what mind can be incarcerated behind such walls of contemplation?

On the days I visited Ukraine, it was always clear that the Government control of the masses was through deprivation. Deprivation of wealth to create a better life for yourself. Deprivation of a mental self-belief in self-worth.

I remember entering the lobby of a hotel in Ukraine. The lights in the lobby consisted of approximately 400 light bulbs arranged in a large square, which was impressive, except that of the 400 bulbs, only approximately 20 were turned on. The effect was draining. Your senses were dulled. Your emotions were dulled. A really interesting experiment on how to engineer others' emotions. A most prosaic way of life.

For much of my time spent in both Russia and Ukraine, I felt as if I was in the Wild West. Life was cheap. Life was expendable. There wasn't much worth living for. Life was for today, not tomorrow.

I remember leaving our office in Kyiv to be driven to my hotel. I heard this clicking sound in the office. Upon enquiring about the same, I was advised that everyone was "tooling up", preparing one's hand-gun for use should the need arise.

Once in the car, I joked that what one really needed was a Kalashnikov. I was advised it was under the seat!

At this time, in the 1990s, I was advised that the going "rate" for an abduction was USD 1,000.00, an assassination….USD 5,000.00! No air miles. I kept this information away from my mother-in-law in case she tried to make a block booking.

Whilst most of my time in Eastern Europe was devoted to Russia and Ukraine, I did venture to the Central Asian Republic of Kazakhstan, a vast country that extends from the Caspian Sea in the West to the Chinese border in the East.

The climate in Kazakhstan ranges from plus 40 degrees in the summer down to minus 40 degrees in the winter.

I visited Kazakhstan to secure steel supplies from a steel mill in a city called Karaganda. Curiously, Karaganda has a German community. This emanates from the time when Stalin transported German prisoners of war from the Russian western front to one of his first prisoner-of-war camps called Karlag. After the war, the freed prisoners just decided to stay in Karaganda.

Kazakhstan is very rich in oil, gas, and mineral resources. A sensible place to erect a steel mill as all your required resources are under your feet.

The steel mill had recently been bought by an Indian conglomerate which proceeded quite naturally to employ Indian personnel in key positions. So, they upped sticks from various parts of the world and amassed in Karaganda together with their wives and families.

Indians really enjoy their own cuisine. Thus, at their own initiative, the wives took over the kitchen of the local hotel and produced some of the most sensational Indian food I have ever tasted. The wives were happy. Their man-folk were delighted. A winning combination!

Pointing the compass southwards, Algeria was different but challenging.

A steel mill in Algeria commenced exports. I arranged to visit the same to procure support for sales to our Southern European markets.

Algeria was a dangerous place to visit. The local Imam had issued a fatwa on all Westerners. Two weeks prior to my arrival, three Russians had been summarily decapitated by a Muslim fundamentalist group whilst walking in the woods one Sunday afternoon.

It is strange to arrive in a new country and immediately be placed under police protection. This consisted of an unmarked police car and two leather-clad policemen who, but for their identity cards, could have been either side of the law,

The unmarked police car was accompanied by a marked police van, so there were a few clues as to where, if not who, we were.

I was forbidden to leave the hotel, and the protection officer slept in the adjacent room!

In the morning, I arrived in the lobby to be escorted to the steel mill. I heard sirens approaching the hotel's front entrance. Here was my ride! Upon strapping myself into my seat, I did raise the question as to whether it was appropriate in maintaining a low profile, that sirens announce my presence!! My concern here was dismissed. Orders had to be followed. Logic took a back seat along with me.

Upon leaving Algeria, my police protection went into fifth gear and took me straight from the entrance to the terminal, through immigration, and through security without a single stop or check. Only when I was in the departure lounge did I wipe the perspiration from my brow and absorb the galactic wind rush.

From the northern shores of Africa, my travels took me westwards to South America.

We already had an established office in Sao Paulo and an agent in Buenos Aires, but this was not sufficient to cover this vast continent.

To enhance our presence in this area, I helped establish offices in both Chile and Columbia.

Let me place into context the importance to us of having offices in South America.

Much of our steel trading centred around our ability to take positions, be they going long or short. To help determine our decision-making process here, we needed to know the price movements of the raw materials which produced the steel, namely iron ore and scrap.

Brazil not only has one of the largest deposits of iron ore in the world, but its quality is also second to none. So, to gather the necessary intelligence to help us determine our position-trading in steel, we needed to embrace trading in iron ore. This was one side of the coin. The other was scrap. Not a particularly romantic product, but critical if we were to "square the circle" and accumulate the necessary intelligence to assist our decision-making process.

So, Brazil was central to our global presence in steel trading. Countries such as Argentina, Chile, Peru, and Columbia complemented our group strategy here.

We did purchase scrap from Brazil, but it had a huge indigenous demand; thus, supply was irregular, and export prices from Brazil were largely determined by what price could be achieved locally.

Chile, however, was totally the opposite. It had no indigenous steel production, so its scrap prices were wholly determined by the price achievable on the international market.

Scrap, to me, was a fascinating product to trade in. It was always a source of amazement to me that owners of scrap yards were basically very honourable people. They were not interested in ripping off customers. They had supplies coming into their yards every day. What they were interested in was turnover. As soon as the scrap was delivered to their yard, they wanted it out.

Scrap yards have their own traditional sources. The importance of this point is that by buying from the same sources, a consistency of quality is both established and maintained. So, from a sales point of view, we, as a trading company, had to know our yards so that we could be comfortable in knowing the type of scrap which we would expect to be supplied. This removed a major source of headache, enabling us to sell the product with minimum concern for quality.

Our trading in South America was not complete without establishing sales outlets for steel products in both Peru and Colombia. We had honourable customers in both markets.

Visits to Bogota were always overshadowed by security concerns. Northern and Central Bogota were relatively safe, whereas the southern part of the city was a little dicey. All business establishments were behind high walls adorned with razor-barbed wire. You never alighted from your taxi outside the premises insisting that you were driven into the compound.

The security guards who patrolled both the inside and outside of the businesses had limited C.Vs. The fact they wore their ammunition as a belt made me wonder what would happen to their trousers if they despatched their full arsenal. Chasing intruders whilst flashing one's "boxers" could have been problematic.

We were soon to resume our habitat abroad by accepting positions in Singapore and then Dubai.

Singapore was an incredible place to work and live. Expensive? Yes, but it was such an efficient working environment. Indeed the whole work ethic was electrifying.

The education system in Singapore was, and still is, rigorous. I found young employees were initially lacking in lateral thinking, but they were quick on the uptake and soon put these same limitations way behind them.

The working day was long. 8 am – 8 pm was not unusual, and once home, the South American markets opened around 11 pm, so one or two calls at that time of night were also not unusual.

The whole Singaporean environment was exciting. You wanted to work. You wanted to achieve. There was an urgency about life. There was no first gear. The pedal of life was flat-down to the floor. The adrenalin just flowed.

Singapore was our Head Office for the Far East including Japan. It has always been an interesting anomaly to me that when talking about the Far East, Japan has never been included in this "umbrella" term. It has always been "Far East and Japan". I am not clear as to the rationale here (if there is any rationale) but I can only surmise that other Far East countries have felt more accessible to the Westerner. Japan certainly does have a strong separate culture and identity and perhaps the English language was not so readily spoken there.

As our H.O., Singapore was a spring-board for my travel to all other Far East countries (including Japan!).

Invariably I was flying to some destination once per week.

If I was to reminisce about one mode of conduct in one Far East country, then it would have to be the experience of crossing the road in Vietnam!!

Vietnam has a population of approximately 98 million who own approximately 50 million motorcycles!

At some point in the day, you would have to cross a road in Vietnam.

You approach the curb and looking to your left, you will see a tsunami of motorcycles. Wave after wave of them. Forget the noise, any conversation with your colleague is not going to happen. Perhaps you think you can cross the road when the lights change? Wrong again as either colour-blindness is endemic in Vietnam or, there is scant regard for any sequencing of illumination.

So, you are still on the curb and witness the monomaniacal, pertinacious expression on the faces of those driving these machines, these motorcycles.

Do not feel the need to attract their attention. They have seen you ten yards before you addressed the curb. So, with no acknowledgement of your existence, you take that leap of faith and step off the curb. This is not the time to reflect upon your life. You take a step and are amazed that a right-angle still exists between you and the tarmac.

Your second step assures you that your musculoskeletal system in your body is still operational. **"NOW"** you shout to yourself, and without trepidation you immediately establish both a constant pace and a focal point across the road where the dangers of this traverse will be but a memory.

"Maintain a uniform pace" you tell yourself and to your utter bewilderment, all the motorcycles take the action necessary to avoid physical contact with you. There is no reduction in speed neither from you nor the cyclists but there has been an immediate calculation in the heads of the motorcyclists involving some co-efficient which ensures you do not assume the position nor pre-determined destination of a projectile.

You arrive safely on the far side, and notch up another pioneering feat.

After Singapore, I worked in Dubai for a friend who owned steel mills in India. He wanted to establish a sales and marketing office to cover the Middle East and North / East Africa.

Establishing an office in Dubai was painful. Yes, you have zero Corporation Tax, but the hoops you have to jump through to obtain the necessary licenses to operate are exhaustive.

Upon arrival, I met our accountant and asked him to list the number of outstanding matters still to be resolved before we could turn the lights on and use the phones. The list extended to one and a half pages and took six months to resolve.

I can see many advantages of working in Dubai, particularly if you are young with a family, but, for me, Dubai holds little attraction.

Sheikh Maktoum, who really is a visionary, has done an incredible job in developing this Emirate. It is a major global hub of commercial activity. Dubai offers people the opportunity to earn money they could never dream of earning in their home countries. It really is a country that can improve your quality of life and that of your dependents but not for me.

I found its ethics challenging.

Shall we leave it at that.

That's a brief global tour of the more interesting places visited.

So, I now come to present to you experiences that have allowed me to draw up a compendium of commercial lessons in life which, in time, you may experience. I hope you will find them interesting, informative, and relevant. Here they are!!

First, some general values.

My career taught me about the value of persistence, resilience, humility, the price to be paid when things do not go to plan, and how one needs to respond to that.

Persistence

One of the biggest compliments I received from a competitor was that John Mainwaring does not go around walls; he goes through them.

It is interesting what can be achieved if one maintains a courteous determination to seek an outcome you fervently believe in.

Let me give you an example.

I had booked an order of galvanized coil to be supplied from Argentina to the UK. The purchase was made in US Dollars, so it was necessary to cover the currency on the purchase side.

After countersignature of contracts, the Argentinian mill nonchalantly advised they would not perform on the contract. Thus, not only was I facing non-performance to a customer, but I had a potential exposure on currency as I would have to cancel the purchase of the USD.

What to do?

The Argentinian mill was not interested in changing its position, insisting that it would not perform. I, therefore, contacted the Argentinian Embassy in London and spoke to their Commercial Attache. I advised him that a nationalized industry in Argentina was reneging on a contract. Is this the image he wished to portray of his country?

I followed up my conversation with the Attache with a personal visit to the Embassy. The next day, I was informed that the contract to supply the galvanized coil had been reinstated.

My potential loss in currency was avoided. Performance was re-established. The day was saved!

May I give you another quite separate example?

I mentioned, in the earlier pages, that I travelled with my colleagues to Siberia every month to book a steel allocation for the USA market. This entailed a flight to Moscow, thence a change to a domestic airport for the flight to Siberia.

We arrived at the domestic airport at 08.00 on a Tuesday morning. Then the games began. Snow fell continuously. However, we were not advised the flight was cancelled. On the contrary, we were advised the flight was delayed by two hours, then another two hours, then another. At 18.00, we were advised the flight would be postponed until Wednesday.

We returned to the airport at 08.00 on Wednesday. Then the games were repeated, so I made the decision that if we were still staring into the Tundra at 12 noon, then we would hot-foot it back to Moscow and catch a train which was leaving at 15.00 for Siberia. At 12 noon, we gathered our bodies and took a taxi to Moscow's main train station. En route, we purchased 6 Mars bars, a bottle of white wine, smoked salmon, and some bread.

We left Moscow at 15.05 and arrived in Siberia at 06.00 (local time), 40 hours later on Friday morning, only to be advised that a plane from Moscow had arrived the previous day!

The persistence we showed to take every possible step to ensure our meetings in Siberia took place was widely respected by the mill. No other company had made an effort to visit the mill that week. Our discussions were very successful. What we set out to achieve was achieved.

Humility

With regard to humility, by its very definition, it is not a value that shouts from the rooftops. I think it is easier to recognise a *lack* of humility.

To me, a degree of humility is absolutely essential to complete one's makeup. Humility denotes an ability to listen and to learn. It also shows reassuring self-confidence.

Let me comment further by turning this point on its head. The *lack* of humility is dangerous. It denotes a person who thinks he knows it all, perhaps fails to admit mistakes, and worse, takes steps to cover them up.

Resilience

In Dubai, one challenge I faced was that I had to create a team from scratch.

I needed a team of approximately ten people to cover: marketing and sales, finance, invoicing, and shipping.

It took me 33 interviews to find three of my team!!

The team I eventually chose was excellent, knowledgeable, motivated, etc., but along the way, I came across some interesting applicants.

One applicant stated in his C.V. that "I get most of my decisions right". So I questioned him about what happened to 49% of the decisions, which were wrong!

I told him I was not going to employ him, but I would spend 20 minutes correcting/improving his C.V. as with such a statement in his C.V., I was pretty sure no one else would.

Persistence, humility, and resilience are all a state of mind. I now introduce you to life lessons drawn from my personal life experiences.

Do Not Be Afraid To Promote Yourself

There is a world of difference between arrogance and over-confidence compared to promoting oneself in a humble, self-effacing, yet determined manner.

At the earliest stage, you need to assess how one gains promotion.

Much of this groundwork could have been covered in your initial interviews, but once you are employed with your feet on the ground, it would be good to assess or re-assess what one has to do to climb the ladder.

Some organizations may have a flat structure, and some may have a more hierarchical structure. Try to verify the type of structure you are in.

In my first "job", it quickly became apparent that to advance within the company, one had to, within one's early years, be posted abroad. Palm trees, Cuba Libres immediately dominated my mindset. To avail myself of this opportunity, I had to "last" a minimum of six months in a department headed by a most ferocious and unforgiving lady. She had the stature of an emaciated bean pole but the lungs of a lioness. Her patience did not qualify her for sainthood.

To enter her department, it was best that you had a belief in premature euthanasia, though I suspect euthanasia is, by its very definition, a state of prematurity.

Having this belief in hand, I walked into her department with the feeling Marie Antoinette had been here before. I advised the lady that although I appreciated that I was not ready to come into her department (an example of humility), being a part of her team was indeed my long-term wish. Within two weeks, I was in her department. My initiation into a world of intolerance, high attainment, and high expectations was about to commence.

Being shouted at, having files thrown around the department, and being mentally pummelled was de rigueur. Our offices were not soundproofed, so we were never able to quantify the audience who availed themselves of these daily histrionics.

My six months tenure in her department soon turned into eighteen months. Tutelage turned into respect. I was obviously a successful clone!

What did I learn? Well, just about everything. I knew nothing prior to my initiation into her department, Humility, hard work, and resilience. I experienced fear. I used to wake up on a Sunday morning thinking about Monday morning. That cannot have been healthy… mentally.

I remember one Monday morning, I arrived at work and threw my daily newspaper on my desk prior to finding the clocking-in machine. Yes, in those days, we were timed in and out of the office. Today this would be deemed an unusual way to assess productivity!! Anyway, before I had time to "clock in", I was called into her room. I can't remember the detail, but I had done something not to her liking. There proceeded a barrage of verbal abuse. One felt well and truly pummelled. After about 10 minutes, I gathered my self-respect and walked out of her office only to be faced with the head of HR advising me that I was late (having failed to clock in!)

After 18 months, I learned all about tough love and a commercial experience that still dwells in the inner chambers of my mind.

Temper Your Ambition To Succeed

If it may bring you into conflict with your boss.

I have to admit there were numerous occasions when, as a young trader, I thought I knew best. If such a sentiment may bring you into conflict with your employer, be careful.

First, there is no harm in expressing your opinion to your boss, particularly if it has been called for. However, if your opinion is in conflict with your boss, tread carefully. Your boss has been employed in a senior position to yourself, has more experience than you and is paid to make decisions. If such decisions grate, hide this emotion. Indeed, support your employer. Especially so if you are asked to implement his decision. He needs to know that his staff is working for him, not against him. If he feels friction here, it may be that your life-span working for him is limited.

Make sure you are part of the solution, not part of the problem.

Establishing a Rapport with Customers and Suppliers.

…...is absolutely critical.

Let's first deal with the initial introduction to a new customer.

When knocking on the door of a new customer, he may well say that he already has well-established sources of supply and does not need you. What is your answer to this?

You do not want to disturb his current purchasing channels…..not yet. But, what you do want to do is persuade him to add your name to the list of his suppliers.

Tell him to carry on booking the bulk of his requirement through his usual channels. This gives him some reassurance that you are not here to disturb his current trade flow. Of course, in reality, your aim is to do just that.

So, whilst giving him some "reassurance" on the one hand, your aim is to persuade him to give you the opportunity to show him both the service and the product which you can supply.

Advising him that you are selling to others in his market is another possible inducement for him to consider purchasing from you.

Once you are in the door, having supplied two or three shipments, then you can go for the jugular and try to supply the bulk of his demand.

Once those initial barriers have been broken down, how is one to proceed?

With both customers and suppliers, you need to try to develop a two-pronged attack. You establish a relationship at one level and seek the assistance of your boss to develop another relationship at a higher level. Should, for some reason, your relationship becomes strained or the decision you are looking for falls outside the ambit of responsibility of your contact, then the second-tier contact can prove extremely useful.

Finding some common ground with the supplier/customer outside of the ambit of work helps develop a close relationship. Football, cricket, or family are good starting points. Most people like to talk about their families. On the business front, you can ask when the business was established and who started it. If it was his father, then you can congratulate him on where the business is today.

When trying to establish a rapport, try to avoid emotive subjects such as....... Brexit. Telling a customer for instance that you were pro-Brexit, may induce an emotive response from him. However, if you turn your comments into a question, "were you in favour of staying or leaving the E.U...." allows you to await his answer and thus enables you to tailor your conversation so that any antagonism is avoided.

Remember, you will do very little business with a person who does not like you.

Upon initially meeting your customer, enquiring about his health is a polite introduction. I used to frequently adopt this line; however, please await the reply from the customer! In my keenness to talk about business, I invariably forgot to await his reply to this question!

If you are in an international environment and your customer is, say, visiting your home country on holiday, make yourself available to him. If he has children being educated in your country, offer your services to him in case of need.

Should you require contracts to be countersigned by either your customer or supplier, choose your moment to secure his/her signature. The contract has essentially already been concluded; thus, you don't want close scrutiny of the written formal agreement. To avoid such a scenario, present the written contract at a time and place when the customer is more relaxed.

In the Caribbean, I used to visit customers on a Friday afternoon, share rum and water with them, and then nonchalantly pull out the contract for signing. The problem with this approach is the amount of alcohol one consumes before attempting to drive back to your office!

Contracts

Whilst commitments will have been reached and agreed upon prior to issuance and countersignature of written contracts, contracts are critical and will contain details not mentioned in the preceding written or verbal exchange.

Here below are some of the more intrinsic paragraphs to be included in contracts. It is difficult to present a complete list here.

Quantity Tolerances:

Any mention of quantity must include tolerances, both negative and positive.

Tolerances on the purchase contract must be tighter than on the sales side. This gives you maximum flexibility.

Tolerances also allow you to take advantage of strengths or weaknesses in the market. If the market is strong and prices are moving up, you want to sell as little as possible but within contracted tolerances. i.e., if you purchase 10,000 MT +/- 10%, you ideally want to ship 9,000 MT and allocate the balance of 1,000 MT to a new order at a higher price. Conversely, if the market is weakening, you want to sell the maximum. In the above example….11, 000 MT.

Description

The description on the purchase contract should be "tighter" and more exact than that detailed on the sales contract.

Shipment/Execution Dates:

These, too, should be tighter on the purchase side than on the sales side. Give yourself at least one month's grace. Purchase May/ June and sell June/July.

Payment Terms with Customer:

These can vary from "open terms" up to the securest form of payment, an irrevocable confirmed letter of credit. If one is giving open terms, it would be prudent to secure credit insurance on the customer. Don't forget to include the cost of such insurance in your profit calculation.

With regard to letters of credit, you need the customer to permit confirmation of the same with a first-class bank in your country. You also need the L/C to permit payment at the counters of your preferred bank. This ensures that you secure payment before the documents are forwarded to the customer's bank.

The Very Existence of a Contract:

In an ideal world, you issue a contract, the customer or supplier countersigns the same, and you then sit back, believing a commitment on both sides exists.

What happens if the supplier/customer does not sign the contract? Re the customer acknowledging a contract, you will not execute the contract until the agreed payment terms have been implemented, but there may be a lapse in time before such implementation.

One way to give you some limited assurance that the supplier/customer acknowledges the existence of a contract is to ask for "shipping marks".

Before any material is transported, be it from a supplier or to a customer, you will need the material to be identified. One way to do this is to place a unique shipping mark physically on the material.

Depending on which party you need the contract to be verified by, ask the same party for a shipping mark. Once the same is in hand, the very fact that they have given you such a mark can be tantamount to prima facie evidence of the acknowledgement of the existence of a contract.

Delegation

This comes later in your commercial life when you have built up a bank of experience.

There is an art to delegating. It is considerably more difficult than one imagines… to do it well.

There is a simple rationale behind the need to delegate. If you don't, then the business can only develop at the speed of one person, you.

If you delegate, then your passing of responsibilities to others allows you to do other things and develop more ideas. This is how companies grow, and those companies where delegation is not actively encouraged will falter or grow at a much slower pace and be left behind.

Certain judgment calls have to be made when delegating. These are not easy to make, and you may well make mistakes here, so be careful.

1) Does the person to whom you are delegating the task have the ability to take on the responsibility you are giving him? Remember that the person you have in mind can hopefully rise to a challenge, so stretch him.

2) Delegation is a two-way street. I always wanted to give as much responsibility to others as I could. This would :

: Maximise the fulfilment of those to whom I delegated.

: Enable the maximum opportunity for growth in the company.

: Hopefully, this would open the door for me to accept additional responsibility, provided those over me were prepared to share the same values as myself.

I like to think that I did indeed give those under me the maximum opportunity to excel. I certainly feel I had a very positive influence on those responsible to me.

But, one word of caution, when handing down responsibility, you need to assess what will fill that gap in your own timetable. Do you have a boss who will also look, in turn, to hand you additional responsibility? Or, is there an opportunity within the company for you to explore new ideas? The point here is, don't lose your power base.

This is a problem I faced. I fully believed, perhaps naively, in the altruistic idea that we all wanted to share as much responsibility as possible to devolve it in any way commercially feasible. This would be a sure way to grow the company and expand its horizons as well as one's own.

I found that some of those with greater responsibility than myself did not hold such an open belief. They very much wanted to keep their current power base. Such a view is, of course, inward-looking and stunts the aspirations for growth, but if people more senior than you hold this view, it is a problem.

Power bases can take the shape of various forms, such as a failure to share contacts, or it can be keeping profit shares for themselves or their section at a cost to the Group's higher aspirations. Such selfish behaviour abounds in companies.

I always held the belief that to make the Main Board, one had to think "Group". Think about what is for the benefit of the Group as a whole, not just one part of it. If one thought in such a way, you still might not be appointed to the Board, but without such an outlook, you certainly would not be worthy of such a position. This philosophy did not always work, although I still think the most successful companies espouse such a thought process.

Let me give you one example.

Through my direct contacts, I could source galvanized steel coils from Vietnam for the USA market. The USA market is the most high-priced market in the world, and to secure such support from any steel mill is difficult.

My colleague in the USA could source the same product directly from Turkey. If he sourced and sold the product, he would secure the whole profit on the order for his office. My request to him was to maintain the Turkish contact but please develop the Vietnamese source. This would have required him to share the profit of the deal, whilst adding another important source to our repertoire.

No one mill (Turkey) can meet all the demand in the USA, a market of 332 million people; thus, there have to be opportunities to also sell the Vietnamese product. Further, if we did not sell the Vietnamese product, then someone else would.

My colleague was not prepared to "share the spoils". We maintained the Turkish source but lost the source from Vietnam. The Vietnamese mill sold into the USA....just not through us.

In a group organization comprising many offices, many egos, and many personal aspirations, the offices which did not think "Group" developed the slowest. There was growth, but not at the rate one would have expected.

Position Trading

This is where you do not have a back-to-back business but are either buying (but not simultaneously selling) in anticipation of the market moving up (going long) or selling (but not simultaneously buying) in anticipation of the market weakening (going short.)

Position trading is not an exact science and is generally perceived to be more risky than back-to-back trading, but this is a misconception.

If you trade back to back, you are committed to both purchases and sales at the same time. Should either the supplier or customer not perform, you are still committed to executing the contract. Believe me, finding an alternative supplier or customer will be costly. However, if one "takes a position", you have the flexibility of where to purchase or sell should you have doubts about performance from the supplier (in the case of a pre-purchase) or the customer (in the case of a pre-sale).

With position-trading, the risk of performance is one-sided. In the case of back-to-back trades, your risk of non-performance is from both sides.

Once a position is taken, you assess what time you have to complete the transaction. If you have pre-purchased, the supplier may state that performance and load readiness will be, say, in two months' time. So, you have two months to sell the material, secure a countersigned contract, and be in receipt of fully acceptable and secure payment terms from the prospective customer.

If you pre-sell, you will have given a latest date in the sales contract by which time you will have contracted to ship the material. So, first, you press for the immediate secure payment terms in your favour. Once in hand, you can negotiate with various suppliers as to when they can make the material load ready for shipment. If, for instance, you need two weeks to arrange a vessel, you work back from the latest date for shipment less the two weeks to arrange a vessel less time it takes for the material to be produced. This gives you the time frame within which you need to book the material.

If you are pre-purchasing, you believe the market is moving upward. If you pre-sell, you believe the market is weakening. How do you determine the movement in the market?

If you have pre-purchased, then you offer material into the market at a price above the level you expect to sell at. If the current sales price is, say, USD 500 MTCF, (Metric Tonne Cost and Freight) then you offer USD 520 MTCF. If customers respond at any level above USD 500 MTCF, then you know the market is remaining strong. So, you negotiate at a price and time frame that permits you to make a margin and ship within the contract. It may be that if price indications are above USD 500 MTCF (in the above example), you do not sell at all in anticipation of the market moving further upwards and wait to offer again into the market at a later date. If the market at that time is, say, USD 530 MTCF, then you are looking at a comfortable margin….but do not be too greedy. If the market shows signs of weakening, which at some time it will, then you probably won't be able to extract any bids from any customer for a period of time whilst the market finds its new lower level.

If the market weakens and say the best price you can achieve is USD 490 MTCF, then you face losing money if you had pre-purchased at USD 500 MTCF. However, all is not lost. You now know first-hand that the market is weakening. Thus, you will need to sell your pre-purchase at a USD 10 MT loss; however, you can pre-sell more material as you know first-hand that the market has weakened.

If you pre-sell and you want to know if the market remains weak, then you send a bid to the supplier at a price below the current estimated purchase price. If the supplier counters with a price idea below the current purchase price, even if above, say, the price you have indicated, then you know the market continues to weaken. If the supplier reverts with a price above your current estimated purchase price, then this is an indication that the market may have turned and is starting to strengthen. In this case, you may lose money on the pre-sale you have taken, but you then pre-purchase more material as you have just received first-hand information that the market has turned and is probably moving upwards.

Remember, you will never be able to predict the exact peak in the market nor the exact trough of the same. For this reason, you need to maintain a constant information flow as to the best price you can purchase at and the best price you can sell at. As advised above, it is not an exact science, but maintaining close contact with both suppliers and customers by respectively regularly offering to buy or offering to sell, are the best and most reliable ways to know the current status of the market.

Ways to Determine Strength in a Market

There are various other ways (apart from those mentioned above) to try to determine the strength of a market. Here are some of them:

High Stocks.

A customer may have high stocks for one of two reasons. Either he is holding onto the same in anticipation of the market moving up, or the market is weakening, and he simply cannot move the same.

If there are high stocks held by either suppliers or customers, then think about the reaction of their bankers. The loans given by the banks against the purchase of materials will have a finite time for repayment. If the supplier or buyer cannot move their material, then they will be under pressure to liquidate their stocks to enable repayment of the bank loans. Such pressure may force a "fire-sale" of material at the "best price".

It is difficult to secure the correct information as to the true level of stock held by a customer to determine the above, but it is a question for which one can at least try to secure an answer.

Strength of Order Book.

This is a really good indicator, but very difficult to secure information thereon. First, determine the usual "lead time" for the supply of an order. This is defined as the time it takes to produce an order. If the supplier has a full order book, then it is likely the "lead time" will be extended. This shows strength in the market. Conversely, if the supplier can produce tomorrow, then obviously, the market is weak and most probably getting weaker.

Developing a New Market

What are the steps you take to develop a new market? You know there is relevant commercial activity in that market, but how do you "get a slice of the action"?

Basically, there are two ways. Either through an agent or direct to the supplier or stockist / end-user depending on whether you are trying to develop a new source or customer base. .

Today, the much-improved communications will steer you to try to go direct to the source or end user. However, what if, for instance, you cannot speak the language of the supplier/customer? There are many parts of the world where your mother tongue may not be freely spoken. In these instances, one may have to consider the use of a third party (agent) to help you penetrate the market.

The use of a third party brings its own problems. For sure, the agent will know the suppliers or customers you are trying to establish contact with, but he is probably working with someone similar to you already. So, where will you be in the pecking order re his loyalty?

Whilst the use of a third party is not ideal (in the circumstances described above), you may not have much choice. Trust will be a major issue, so a market visit should be a priority so that you can be introduced directly to the supplier / end user face-to-face.

Of course, no self-respecting agent will agree for you to communicate directly with the supplier/end-user, but direct communication has to be your ultimate goal for as long as the agent also works for others, your competitors.

In time, if you foresee long-term business, then you will want to establish your own office in that location.

I am painting broad strokes here, but the principle of "as direct a communication as possible" has to be the endgame.

Claims / Debt

I combine Claims / Debt together because there can be adverse reactions from customers in both situations.

I will deal with Claims first.

When presented with a claim, your first thought must be… there is money to be made here.

Let me approach this subject from two angles. First, understanding where the claimant is coming from. Second, handling the specifics of the claim.

With regard to understanding the claimant, I believe there is great value to try to get inside his head.

Why is he making this claim? The rationale may, of course, be totally clear where, for instance, you have supplied the wrong material completely. But perhaps the rationale is not so clear. Look at the environment surrounding the making of the claim. Is the market strong or weak? The vast majority of claims are made when the market is weak or getting weaker. The claimant has, say, purchased material, but his market for selling the material has dropped, so he is facing making a loss. One way to try to recoup his loss is to make a claim on his supplier!

Try to understand where he is coming from. Claims per se can be confrontational, but if you can understand where the claimant is coming from (but not necessarily agree with his logic), then you go some way to creating an atmosphere of reasonableness between you both. Indeed, there can be substantial merit in advising the claimant that you understand his position. You can then present your case as to why you differ from his proposed outcome.

Another reason, and there are many, of course, could be that the material does not look good. It may say look rusty, and he uses this as a basis for his claim even if the rust does not adversely affect the performance of the material.

Even where there appears to be justification for a claim, it may well be covered by any reasonable insurance policy, so why has the customer claimed on you and not through his insurance policy? The answer may be quite simple, he does not want to claim upon his insurance and thereby increase his premiums for years to come.

There is logic in the above, but such logic can "cost" you.

So, one solution is why not purchase with insurance covered by the supplier. In this case….you! In this way, you take the hassle off the shoulders of the customer. The rates that an insurance company charges you may be very competitive compared to rates quoted in many third countries.

Whilst one never wants to be over-keen to make a financial settlement, dragging one's feet with a customer who has a justified claim can cause irreparable damage to your relationship with him. If he has a complaint, he would like to know that upon receipt of the same, you are not running at a million miles an hour into the sunset.

On the contrary, prompt settlement can produce huge long-term dividends. It is always a question of degree and judgment.

Also, please remember what you settle for with the customer has little or no bearing on the settlement you reach with the supplier. They are two totally different transactions.

The timing of your settlement with the customer should not necessarily be dependent upon the response, or lack thereof, from the supplier. Of course, one should try not to be "out of pocket", but if you have acted as a principal with your customer, then he is not interested in whether you have reached a settlement with your supplier. That's your business, not his. He wants a prompt settlement; thus, if there are justified grounds for the same, strike the settlement and move on, hopefully to new business though perhaps from a different supplier.

Every effort should be made to ensure that upon the settlement of a claim, a relationship still exists with your customer for business to continue. He may not want the financial settlement to be intrinsically attached to the new business, but once a settlement has been reached, every possible effort should be made for the new business to be booked. There is not much point in reaching a settlement with a customer if he never wants to see you again!

A claim settlement has to resolve the issue at hand, but it is imperative that it does not prevent new business from being booked. Don't accept the customers' word for it. Try to book the new business there and then. It is not an unreasonable request.

You should not discount the option of presenting a claim against a supplier without an actual claim being lodged by the customer!

I remember one incident where the customer lodged a claim for poor galvanizing of a product. Coating claims (for which this is one) are notoriously difficult to prove against a supplier. However, in this instance, the supplier actually supplied material outside of the chemical parameters permitted within the grade. We, therefore, lodged a claim accordingly though we never received such a claim from the customer! In the end, we settled with the customer, but part of the financial settlement we received from the supplier related to the chemical analysis claim for which no official claim had been received!

One final point about claims. Even if you are successful in refuting the basis of the claim, try not to leave the customer with a loss of face. This is a very subjective point. If he has tried to "rip you off" from the start, then one can be "hard-nosed" with some justification, but if he has appeared reasonable throughout......but "lost", then you may want him to salvage some pride. This can be done in various ways (slight reduction in price next order etc. etc.). It is gesture economics!!!

With regard to Debt, I will comment from the positions of both creditor and debtor.

From the position of creditor, extracting debt though the lawyers / courts can be extremely expensive, time consuming and without guarantee of a satisfactory outcome. If the debtor is receptive to acknowledging his debt and receptive to a dialogue on the same, then that is a result in itself. With regard to recovery of the debt, it may well be worthwhile emphasising to the debtor that part payments would be acceptable. You then want to try to agree a rescheduling of the debt detailing a specific time frame.......and agreed amount to be paid each month. Of course ideally, interest should also be recovered but in my experience this is a concession which plays well with the debtor. You are seen to "give" something to him.....in return, you expect the capital amount to be paid in full.

From the position of a debtor, if you are serious about preserving your reputation and effecting a repayment, then if repayment of the whole amount "in one go" is too much to contemplate, then offer a staggered repayment schedule. There is a colossal difference in the eyes of a creditor between paying nothing at all and being prepared to pay an agreed amount in instalments. The former places you firmly in the camp of **bad** debtors whilst the latter shows a bona fide attempt to:

A) Recognise the existence of a debt.
B) Do something about settling it.

Try to keep lawyers at bay.

Communication

If you were to summarise the qualities required for most careers in business/commerce, then I would say: common sense, a good memory, and an ability to communicate would be the top three.

After Singapore, I spent just over two years in Dubai. The task at hand was to establish a marketing arm for an Indian steel mill. The office I established was multicultural, both by design and by chance. India, Morocco, Lebanon, the Philippines, UK were all represented out of a total staff number of 10!

A multicultural environment, whilst it enriches your own being, can present its own challenges. First and foremost, communication.

With international communication, be it verbal or written, be aware that you may be communicating with people whose first language is not English. Thus, be mindful of how you express yourself, as there is always a danger of misinterpretation.

I had an instance where in response to his colleague, who was not familiar with English idioms, the person in question exclaimed, "Oh Boy!" To those of us conversant with such an expression, such a phrase would equate to "Wow". However, to the person in question, he believed he was being referred to as a "boy", which he considered derogatory.

In another instance, an employee in the UK stated that a situation was so common that "every man and his dog" would know it. The recipient, of Middle East descent, believed he was being called a dog and took great exception.

Be careful. However precise are the words or phrases which you use, if they contain a word that in another context would be deemed offensive, the recipient of such a comment may not spend the time or effort to decipher the phrase and only see an objectionable word even if the specific context in question could not reasonably be deemed offensive.

Remember, you are the master of the unspoken word!

Another lesson in communication. In many cultures, you will come across the admirable quality of someone not wanting to disappoint you. This may be promising performance on a quite peripheral subject, or it could be of a more serious nature where say, you need performance as part of a contractual obligation. In other words, you have to disseminate when "yes" means "no".

In my international travel, I came across several instances where customers or suppliers did not want to give me a negative reply. They wanted to feel that they could provide all solutions to the problem facing me. They were not purposely trying to be deceptive but took great personal pride in being able to be of assistance to me. Thus, the question here is if you suspect that their reply does not provide the solution, how do you extract a more meaningful reply from them?

The answer is that you need to give them the opportunity to "save face". So, to give a simple example, if you are told that "the goods will definitely be supplied tomorrow", you perhaps state, "whilst we hope the goods will be supplied by tomorrow, we understand that the supplier has experienced many difficulties in production so we suspect that there could be a delay in the delivery schedule. Have you heard the same?" This immediately gives the person you are in conversation with the opportunity to tell you the real situation without loss of face, as YOU have already created the environment where a negative reply is both plausible and half expected.

Do Not Guarantee the "Arrival" of Material

Do not guarantee the arrival of any product. You will no doubt have to commit to a latest shipping date. This is not unreasonable, but to guarantee an arrival date is foolhardy.

You have no control over the weather or any force majeure situation which may befall you; thus, stay away from this "trap".

On the contrary, be careful with a customer who has made this request. It is neither serious nor commercial to request a guarantee of arrival of material; thus, such a request may divulge more about the character of the customer than he intended.

Increase in Customs Duties – An Opportunity?

When a country raises import duties, the natural reaction is to think that such action will inhibit imports. i.e., curb the exports you are trying to execute.

That is not necessarily the case.

When a government increases import duties, look at the reaction from domestic manufacturers.

George W. Bush, when President of the USA, announced an increase in duty on hot rolled steel coil from Russia to the USA. The increase was in the region of 20%. Such an increase would kill off all such imports, or so you would think. In fact, the opposite happened.

When import duties increased, imported goods became more expensive. Thus, local (domestic) manufacturers took this as an opportunity to make more profit and increased their own domestic prices to the consumer. The increase that domestic producers imposed on their customers totally negated the increase in import duty. As a result, imports continued, albeit at higher prices higher, but still competitive compared to increased domestic prices.

Rights and Wrongs

Remember, if you are involved in a conflict with a supplier or customer, it is one thing to be morally, ethically, and contractually "in the right." However, if your adversary is holding the funds relating to the conflict or has exclusive access to them (to the exclusion of yourself), then who is in the right? Does it matter?

Perhaps down the line, it does, but fighting a legal battle and winning is not your top priority at this stage. Your top priority is to ensure your interests are protected, and that invariably means you have unfettered access to the funds in question.

Control the money. Control the funds, and then you can control the situation.

Rule of Law

Every contract will specify a legal franchise that will govern the interpretation of the contract in the event there is a legal dispute.

Should one reach the legal stage in a dispute, it will be costly and, from a commercial point of view, unlikely to have a happy ending.

I remember we had a case of non-performance from a customer in South America. We won the arbitration in the UK, and we secured the South American courts' approval to enforce the arbitration. Unfortunately, when we came to "knock on the door" of the customer, he was not there. He had also disposed of his assets. It cost us GBP 140,000.00 to secure the arbitration and the rights to enforce it. We got nothing.

Respect for a Country's Customs

Be aware of the environment you are working in. Be mindful of the local customs and traditions. You want to avoid, at all costs, your behaviour being interpreted as an affront to the values held by your customer or supplier.

Ramadan

If you are meeting members of the Muslim faith during the month of Ramadan, then you must remember that during the hours between sunrise and sunset, Muslims do not partake of any food or liquid.

I remember visiting a customer in Sudan. He invited me into his office and politely offered me a drink. With 51 degrees C outside, I heartily accepted the same. During consumption of the same, I witnessed my customer forlornly looking at me. It was only then that I realised how insensitive I had been. Thereafter, I took a cooler in the car and had a drink before I entered the customer's office. This enabled me to reject his kind offer of some sustenance and show respect for the norms exercised during the month of Ramadan.

Pujah

This is a Hindu ceremony celebrated once per year. It manifests itself in the blessing by a Hindu priest of the customers' new order books.

Once the books are blessed, the customer wants to write new orders into his books. To participate in this ceremony, one is requested to make an offer of material. The quantity is more symbolic than commercial, but the customer is obliged to accept whatever price you offer to him, with no negotiation. So, please banish all thoughts of making a good margin on such sales. The customer will book whatever price level you give him, but if he feels he has been ripped off, he will remember!!!!

Chinese New Year

Such celebrations can last from one week up to one month, generally the former.

This is a joyous occasion whereby you visit the offices of your customers/suppliers and wish them good fortune in the year ahead.

Be prepared to extend your imagination as to the type of food which will be offered to you and the copious amounts of alcoholic drinks which will be placed before you from 09.30 until well after sunset! Your kidneys will need a rest after this.

If You Made a Mistake, Front It Up. Admit It

We all make mistakes.

If you believe you are responsible for a mistake, tell your boss. He will have delegated certain responsibilities to you. He needs to feel comfortable that he has made the right decision here. Walking into his office to make him aware of an error shows, to him, not only that you have the courage to own up to a mistake but also shows that you have confidence in yourself.

The early admission of a mistake allows the company to address it immediately. Whatever the cost of remedying it, it will be cheaper than if you try to hide the error.

Mistakes will always "come out" in the end. If you are belatedly found out to be responsible, then as a boss, I will always be wary of you in the future. What else are you hiding? What are other errors waiting to be discovered? Front it up. Take the punishment, if any, but at least you have been honest, and move on.

Even if you have been admonished for making a mistake, take it on the chin. Your pride will be hurt, but there is not a person around you who has not been in that position.

Your superiors and peers will be looking to see how you react to being "the culprit". Do not make light of it but quickly put it into perspective. Yes, some cost will be involved, but it happens in every field of life. Show you can shoulder the responsibility for the error but move on to the next task at hand.

You will come across people who do not admit their errors. Who cannot bring themselves to say "sorry"? Don't be one of them.

It does not matter how many times you get knocked down, it is how you **get up** that matters.

Honesty with Customers

The most awkward question a customer can ask you is: "What should I do?" "Should I buy or not?" Yet here you are on a mission in life to **sell**!!!

In these situations, you have to be scrupulously honest with the customer.

If you told the customer to buy at a time when the market was weak, and the prices did indeed drop further, what would he think of you in the future? He would give scant acknowledgement of your advice.

Best to be honest. If the market is weakening, tell him to wait to buy.

There is another good reason, to be honest. He probably has doubts about the strength in the market in any case and is just looking for confirmation of a view he probably already holds!!

Be honest, and your long-term relationship with him will only be the better for it.

Don't Lie

Apart from any moral or ethical issues you may have here, telling a lie can define you in the eyes of your colleagues or suppliers/customers for eternity.

Being "commercial" with the truth, not giving a person the full picture, is just about acceptable, but lying………stay away from this temptation. Apart from anything else, for every word of a lie, you will need ten words to cover it up. You will also need an extremely good memory!! Just don't go there.

Speeches

Whenever you have to make a speech in a foreign country unless you are fluent in the language of the host country, I suggest that you speak in your natural tongue but make your initial comments, including a thank you for the invitation to speak, in the language of the host country. Such a gesture is always highly appreciated and sets a very positive tone for your presence there. Hand-write the introduction, and by all means, use phonetic spelling so that the pronunciation sounds authentic.

The speech in the foreign language only needs to be short, and you can end it by saying (in the foreign language) that "……you are no doubt giving them a headache so, with respect, you will return to speaking English….."

Think – Write – Rethink – Transmit

There will be occasions when you are writing an important document (as opposed to, say, a cursory email reply).

If the content of your email MAY have ramifications, then draft it, but then DO NOT send it immediately.

Sit on it for a day. Read it a few times. Be assured that every time you read it, you will most definitely be able to improve the syntax, if not the content.

Only when time has elapsed (one or two days) and you have read it, say 5 – 10 times, should you then transmit the message.

In this way, you have given yourself time to rationally assess both the content and tone of the message.

In this way, you avoid any possible regrets in conveying your point of view including any emotive comments. Emotional comments always tend to debase the point or argument you are trying to make.

You Are Not an Island

You will need the co-operation of others to succeed. When you are assessing the need for the co-operation of a third party, take a moment to assess how best to secure this.

In the 1980s, Jamaica had serious foreign exchange issues. When you, as an exporter to such a country, require payment for goods supplied (outside of a letter of credit), then once the customer has paid his local currency into his bank, one does not expect any delay in the remittance of the foreign exchange.

Not true.

If the central bank has limited access to foreign exchange, then your customer's remittance will join a queue for the expatriation of funds.

Once a month, on my travels to Jamaica, I would visit the Bank of Jamaica, the central bank which held all the country's foreign exchange. On one occasion, I met the Governor himself. Did this help in the remittance of forex? Frankly. No. However, I met Mrs Harrison, his secretary, and whilst I am the first to admit that my charm has limitations, I struck a chord with Mrs Harrison, who ensured that our customer's application for forex was at the top of the pile for the Governor's signature.

Knowing the Governor sounded good at cocktail parties, but it was Mrs Harrison who got the job done!

Can You Help Me?

How disarming can such a request be?

I was trying to book business with a subsidiary of a major group in Trinidad.

Whatever price or terms we offered, we could not book any business. This status persisted for months.

What to do?

If I did nothing, this vacuum of commercial activity would persist. I, therefore, decided to seek a meeting with the Chairman of the holding company on the basis that we had absolutely nothing to lose.

At the meeting, I made the Chairman aware of our past attempts to conclude business etc. etc. and asked if he "could help me".

Approximately ten days later, I was advised that the M.D. of the subsidiary company had been dismissed.

At a subsequent meeting with the Chairman, he asked me why I thought he had listened to me. He relayed to me that when I asked if he "could help me", it reminded him of a request he made to a Canadian bank when he asked them if they "could help" him…which they duly did in providing finance.

"Can you help me" …it's a nice turn of phrase in such delicate situations.

Food

International business requires international travel and a taste for international cuisine!!

With regard to the latter, goat's gizzards, fish's stomach, duck's tongue, meat preserved in wax, and sea cucumbers, maybe a few of the delicacies one is compelled to eat to avoid offending one's hosts.

In Taiwan, I found myself eating a fish's stomach! Having survived the experience, I arrived back at my hotel, went to my room, prepared myself for bed and promptly fainted! I woke up in a pool of sweat from head to toe, but strangely, I felt fine.

Wherever you find yourself, if a customer or supplier is prepared to spend time eating with you, it has to be a good sign.

Being able to consume alcohol is not obligatory, but it can help though nothing will compare to giving your host a good price for what he or she is looking to buy/sell.

In Ukraine, raw pork fat was a delicacy enjoyed by one customer. You eat it in the autumn to fatten you up for the winter! One may protest that one's girth was already "ample", not a chance. I never came so close to being force-fed.

How to Handle Staff When You Are the "New Kid on the Block"

How do you enmesh yourself into an established team?

How do you establish yourself as the "Team Director"? Yes, you hold the title, but how do you ensure everyone is on side, on your side? The bottom line is that not everyone may want to be "on your side". Your appointment may have caused certain resentment within the team. That aside, how do you establish your identity and authority?

Initially, you will draw your own prompt gut feelings about the individuals in your team. These gut feelings will cover both positive and negative sentiments.

Let's deal with the negative ones.

Someone in your position or higher, employed the people now working for you. They made assessments and found the people worthy of the position they are now holding. You, however, may have a different opinion.

The first lesson here is to be patient. You do not want to be making rash personal judgements. This will unsettle the team and produce negative feelings against you. This, when you have just moved into the position you are now holding.

You should believe that in every person working for you, there must be some good. Your job, as a manager, is to find that "goodness" and let it shine through for the benefit of the person and the Company.

Having stated the above, do not completely abandon your own gut feeling if you think a person is not right for your team.

I faced a situation once where one of my team advised me that every Wednesday, he had lunch with some major end-users who "held court". It was, therefore, critical that he be there and secure market intelligence. So, every Wednesday, he was absent from the office but supposedly gaining good information for the betterment of the Company.

I was initially sceptical about the value of such meetings, but one cannot just dismiss these arrangements, particularly if they have been ongoing.

In my mind, I gave the person in question 8 weeks. I indulged him for eight weeks. After this time, I felt empowered to challenge him to show me the value of such meetings. What specific bookings had emanated from these meetings?

None.

I was offered a diatribe about how important it was for our company to be seen at such gatherings. This statement led me to believe that perhaps my colleague was actually doing a lot of talking at such meetings with a view to impress all attendees.

The lesson here is that I placed the person in question in a position whereby HE had to justify the lunches by the size of his order book. I don't think he was ever used to sandwiches at his desk on Wednesdays!

With regard to those who create a positive impression from the start, just be wary of those who overtly go out of their way to impress you.

And, don't forget the quiet ones who just get on with their job. Though, they shouldn't be too quiet. The ability to communicate should not be compromised.

Once you have your team, even if there are dying embers of reluctance, you have the basis for building a strong rapport within that team.

Take an interest in every individual who makes up that team, not just an interest in the high-profilers. Get to know them personally. Get to know what makes them tick including their own concerns. Over the years, I had people working for me who:

: Were going through an unrelenting adoption process.

: Needed bereavement counselling due to the unexpected death of his best friend.

: Abuse by a boyfriend.

: Required psychiatric help due to being involved in a train crash.

With regard to the psychiatric help, I arranged for the company to pay such costs.

Outside of specific problems such as the above, I engendered a culture of hard work, integrity, and fairness whilst maintaining a good sense of humour throughout with my staff.

I bought them all one drink and a plate of chips every Friday lunchtime. It brought about such a good feeling amongst us all. I am not saying every day was paradise. When mistakes were made, I did haul up those concerned, but the tough talk was even more poignant compared to the general positive vibe that persisted amongst the teams.

On the trading front, allow the team to "cut their teeth". I remember one young steel trader booking his first order with a German steel mill. The price he gave the mill was frankly higher than was probably necessary, so, on paper, we left some profit on the table, but at what cost? What was important here? Yes, I could have made more money for the Company if I had taken over the reins of negotiation, but how would the young trader have felt? Deflated? Self-esteem dented? By allowing him to determine the outcome, it gave him confidence that he could tuck under his belt and "bank" it for the future.

May I add just one more paragraph here as it relates to your relationship with your staff. My message is this:

At the end of the week, make sure all members of your staff leave with a smile on their faces. Whatever the problems and pitfalls which have befallen them throughout the last week, do not let them carry these problems out of the office. They stay firmly in the office. Yes, these problems will still have to be dealt with next Monday but next Monday your staff will be refreshed and they can look at all these problems with a new face.

Somehow, the problems will be solved, but brooding over them will not help solve the problem…..nor will it help your staff. They need to return to office on the Monday exhilarated, energised, invigorated and "ready to go"! Melancholy… be banished.

Where Taking Action Against an Employee May Bring You into Conflict with the Law

There are approximately 250 working days in a year.

I once had the misfortune to employ a person who worked approximately 160 days a year. You name the reason, and the person in question would take a day off.

"The dog is ill".

"My parent's dog is ill".

"My car was broken into".

"My parent's car was broken into".

You give the person notice in writing, and they immediately attend work and behave. However, after a few months, your written notice is diluted in its threat of disciplinary action. The person knows this, so after a few months, the "games" begin again.

What to do?

You are a corporation against one "vulnerable" person. The optics do not look good.

We took the view that those working around the person in question saw a person who was able to "take the p*ss" and get away with it.

Rightly or wrongly, we decided to summarily dismiss the person and "take the hit" should we ever be taken to a tribunal.

We never heard from the person again.

Interviewing

Acquiring the right personnel is one of the most critical functions within any company or enterprise.

It was accepted that my interviewing technique was a little "off the wall".

Frankly, when interviewing, I paid scant attention to the academic qualifications scribed on the tablets before me. I knew the person in front of me was intelligent, or else he/she would not have passed the first hurdle with our HR department. But what I wanted to know was the person... the personality behind the suit or dress.

Most of the questions I wanted to ask are forbidden today. However, one can glean good introspective detail by asking certain pertinent though polite questions.

Here are some examples:

**Do they have siblings? If yes, are they the oldest or the youngest? You find the former had a harder time growing up and the latter to be "the baby" of the family.

**Some interviewees mention passing certain grades in exams, i.e. 6 GCSEs in Grades A-C. When asked how many were in Grade A, one hopeful advised, "None". A little deceptive, I believe. The interview was terminated forthwith.

**What do their parents do? This gives you an insight into their background and values together with any hardships.

**Any life-changing experiences? One lady I interviewed hoped to be a ballet dancer, but a car accident put an end to such aspirations. She was now applying to become a steel trader... so she faced a devastating accident, regrouped, picked herself up and now looked to pursue a career with us. Such tenacity. Guts. We hired her.

I interviewed one gentleman who was captain of the first XV rugger team at school. Good bloke, I thought. We hired him, but then he appeared to be lacklustre to the tasks set before him. He resigned to return to his father's travel business, but I questioned myself....where did I go wrong in thinking he had the qualities required for the job? ....and then I realised I had failed to ask one question....he was captain of his first XV, but... did his team win? Perhaps he was not such a good captain...... perhaps.

Another gentleman presented himself in a suit and tie. The tie had a huge "smiley" face on it. The interview proceeded. He ticked many of the boxes, and then I asked him, "Do you think it was a good idea to wear such a tie to an interview?" He replied, "Probably not". We hired him, but the reason I asked the question was not to doubt his right to wear such a tie but to question his judgement. Is an interview the right place to impose your taste in clothing? Get the job, and then perhaps you can determine your own dress code..... perhaps..

Impressions

There may be times when customers want to impress you with their worldliness, their knowledge, their power, and their money. My advice here is …. be guarded. You can congratulate them. However, there can be lessons to be learnt from such aggrandisement.

I had a customer in the Far East who owned steel mills and hotels etc. etc... One night, I was leaving our local office to catch the plane back to Singapore when he called requesting that we meet urgently in one of the hotels he owned. This was going to be tight as local city traffic was horrendous, and my flight was the last out that night.

I agreed to meet, and discussions proceeded. All was good except I was left with a journey of one and a half hours to the airport with my flight in two hours' time.

After our meeting, I went down into the hotel lobby to be confronted with three police motor bikes surrounding my office car. I wondered what the fuss was about… perhaps some celebrity in town? No. This was my ride!!

My customer had arranged for the city police force to give me three police out-riders!! So, my driver, having been requested to put on his warning flashing lights, drove me, escorted, post haste to the airport, a trip which would normally take one hour and a half took me 30 minutes.

Was I impressed? Mightily. However, take a check on reality here. If this customer has such influence over the police, what influence can he exercise over the judiciary should you ever have a legal conflict with him?

Receiving the Benefit Of The Doubt

Until you get to know someone, human nature is such that one will generally give that person the benefit of the doubt as to the views they hold. It is a subconscious respect for the unknown.

I have been the recipient of this respect in many situations.

Having your views, your very presence "immortalised" is indeed flattering but be careful. Do not usurp this privileged position.

Not only must your views be sound, but you must conduct yourself in a way becoming that of a person who has the respect of others.

Holding a point of view which subsequently becomes erroneous due to events outside of your control will not lessen your credibility but should your own conduct be questioned, i.e. conduct unbecoming, then your esteemed position may well be brought into question.

Once that respect has been lost, it is probably lost… for good.

Nurture it. It is an invaluable asset.

Travel – If You Have The Opportunity… Grab It

Travel broadens your horizons. It is part of your education in life. It exposes you to:

*different values,

*different experiences,

*different cultures,

*different codes of conduct,

*different norms

All of which enrich your life.

Be the Best

Whatever responsibility you are given as you step through life, make sure you know everything there is to learn about it.

My background is in steel trading, so as an example, at one time, I was given the responsibility of selling wire rods from Turkey to the Middle East. This would involve:

a) Knowing every possible customer.

b) Knowing our competition.

c) How is the material imported?

d) What import licences are involved?

e) What are the duties levied?

f) Are certain qualities imported without import duty?

g) Is the wire rod converted into products for export?

h) Can we get involved in the export?

i) etc. etc. etc.

Let me give you another example:

As previously advised, I lived in India for three years. A thoroughly enjoyable three years. During that time, my company was importing tinplate (used for making cans) from the UK to India. Our customers were end-users.

India had a very complicated import licence structure which levied large import duties on the imported product. To avoid or reduce the import duty, our customers used a certain category of licence not generally utilised for such imports. These licences enabled the customer to import under a lower tariff, so the cost of the material, after customs duty, was cheaper. Thus, when customers complained about our prices (which they would do as a matter of course!), we could negate their argument by highlighting the availability of import licences which attracted the lower duty.

The point here is that we could only present such an argument or justification if we ourselves had knowledge of the import procedures and licence structure.

Knowledge is power indeed.

Culture Shock… and Reverse Culture Shock!

Culture shock manifests itself when you are moving to a different country. However "civilised" that new country has appeared in your mind prior to your arrival, your very arrival will produce mixed emotions within you.

The adjustment required to accept life in a different culture can be invigorating, exciting, and stimulating. It can also be unsettling and alienating. Perhaps a different sense of humour is required. One thing is for sure… it will be a test of character.

In the early days, keep as open a mind as possible. Your adjustment to your new surroundings will be greatly assisted if you can mix the old with the new. If you are working, this is easier as, for the most part of the day, you will be in an environment where one's communications are relatively familiar… you may, for instance, be talking to some of the same people as prior to your arrival in your new surroundings. Such a benefit may not be accorded to your partner. Therefore, be sensitive to the needs of the latter.

You most probably cannot make a total and immediate transition to your new environment. Thus, do not expect miracles. You need to wake up in the morning in as positive a frame of mind as possible to help the transition, and there is no shame in seeking out others from your country of origin. Joining a club of ex-patriots is not unusual and provides a base and a refuge for those moments when the pressure of the new environment becomes too taxing.

One tip for the new arrivals….try to appreciate the differences between the new and the old, which in time, repeat in time, will create the euphoria and the challenges which you will hopefully embrace.

What is surprising to experience, though, is reverse culture shock, i.e. when your term abroad has finished, and you return "home".

Such experiences can be equally difficult to adjust to, particularly if the time abroad has been measured in years.

The first challenge is acclimatising to the UK weather. Whilst I am certainly no doctor, UK clouds and rain can invariably necessitate a regular course of vitamin D.

When abroad, I always felt that I was a pioneer. New culture, new dress code, new working hours (invariably longer), and new sounds all extended an invitation to absorb, take stock, accept and enjoy. Upon my return to the UK, the pioneering spirit went AWOL. There was a sameness about life. People were perfectly polite and engaging, but your subconscious thirst for challenge went… well, unchallenged.

Old values were re-ignited. Your identity perhaps became less pronounced. As an ex-patriot, your skin colour and/or your voice, your mindset made you distinctive. Back home, such distinctions became the norm. A spice in life was missing.

Repeating one's experiences abroad to other ex-patriots met with a certain resonance which was missing with those not versed in such challenges. No criticism here for those who crusaded over London Bridge for much of their successful working life, but one is just trying to rationalise the differences one faces upon return to the UK or, I suspect, return to any "home" life.

Coping with a Negative Frame of Mind

My father once told me, "Life is not always beer and skittles". You hit the dark times. How do you cope and come out the other side feeling good about yourself or at least able to cope with the challenges which befall you.

No way am I a psychologist. Nor do I have any medical training, but let us approach this problem from a pragmatic, common-sensical point of view.

Let's try to develop some broad principles together so that we can arm ourselves against the bad times and enjoy the good times.

The very worst scenario is where you feel despondent and discouraged. Wow. How often do you read in the national press that someone, usually a film star, "felt suicidal"?

Well, hello. Who hasn't in their lifetime felt, to some extent, depressed? I have. I have felt so down that I believed I could have used a fracking licence. But I believe most of us have been lucky to find that morsel of mental strength to retain a survival perspective on life.

I will never forget the line in Crocodile Dundee when Hogan was advised someone had committed suicide. "Didn't he have any mates?" was his question. To me, it sounds like a pretty rational question to ask. There is just one problem, people contemplating suicide are not, I would submit, thinking rationally.

I cannot really comment further on such as state of mind, nor should I. This is a field of expertise I do not possess. So, let us look at situations which are important to us but do not push us to consider the direst of consequences.

You are put into a dark place primarily because an event or maybe two or three events have happened simultaneously or someone has said something to you which has upset you.

If it is the former, my instinct would be to call a friend to see if they can help you. Even if they cannot give you physical help, their comments may help you to regain some composure and perspective to enable you to tackle the problem.

If it is the latter, where things have been said which upset you, how do you deal with this?

I have encountered two typical responses to this latter scenario. The first is where the recipient just absorbs the insult, suppresses any impulse to respond and just moves on in life. The second response is where the recipient raises hell about the incident and tells everyone about the incident except the very person who caused the upset!

I have found that the majority of people shy away from confrontation. They prefer to take the insult "on the chin" and move on. If you are happy to be treated in this way then who am I to question your actions? However, may I make two observations here?

1) If a person has talked to you in a disparaging way, they will not respect you. That is a fact. If you can live with this …fine, but you have your pride, your self-respect, your self-esteem. Where are those values if you allow someone to treat you with such disdain?

2) If you can't live with the situation, then what to do? The incident is "eating you up ". It is uppermost in your thoughts throughout your day and night. It affects your mood, your judgement, your relationships with others. If you do nothing then this state of affairs will persist….and what a miserable state of affairs it is. So, let me ask one question…why should you endure this torment? Particularly when the perpetrator is probably totally oblivious to your self-inflicted anguish.

There is only one thing to do. At some time in some way you will need to confront the person. My use of the word "confrontation" is not to insinuate a military style manoeuvre! But, you will need to talk directly to the person involved. This is an uncomfortable position for most people because most people do not relish such an encounter but, there are some times in your life when you have to take a stand and we are here, now, discussing such a time.

I have been in this situation on more than one occasion.

Do not lose your composure. Do not dramatise the situation …nor should you make light of it. Maintain an unemotional, balanced even detached voice. Do not make any humorous comment but simply, without embellishment, tell the culprit the reasons why you are upset.

I cannot list here the responses you should give in response to their reply to you but just state your case. If they apologise then, you cannot ask for more. If they do not apologise then you can register your utmost regret that they did not think it appropriate to apologise….and leave it at that. You have stated your case. You cannot do more but you will feel good about yourself and you will be proud of yourself. You will also probably have gained their respect, but don't expect them to tell you that.

Be Yourself

Believe in yourself. If you do not have confidence in yourself, you cannot expect others to have confidence in you.

Your lack of self-confidence will show, and others may take advantage of this.

This may mean you have to "pump yourself up"....give the impression to others of confidence in your own ability at a time when really all you want to do is curl up into a ball.

To help you regain your confidence, latch onto something which boosts your self-esteem. For me, I get a great kick out of learning new conventions in Bridge, a game I took up only three years ago. The fact that I may not be able to recognise the conventions when they hit me in the face is immaterial!! Just the new knowledge entering my head gives me a kick. The other booster of my self-esteem is reading non-fictional books. I am not an intellectual, but gaining new information about people or events is a great fillip for me.

Earlier, I said... "Be yourself". What I am saying here is not a contradiction to this. The world is not fair, and human nature is such that there will be those out there who want to test your resolve. Showing self-confidence is a good defence mechanism against those who may feel inclined to seek out your weaknesses.

You're better than them. Make sure it shows.

Don't try to be someone you are not. This will cause too much mental stress upon yourself. Don't be concerned about what others think of you. Of course you should be mindful of others and retain a degree of civility towards them but first and foremost if you want to build a relationship with them make sure they respect you and your views. Respect comes before friendship. Friendship may be a goal that is attainable but don't think you have a friend without them first respecting you.

Do Not Be Embarrassed by Your Lack of Knowledge

It may be that you are in discussions with a customer or supplier where your knowledge of the subject matter in question is limited.

It is perhaps contrary to human nature to admit to a lack of knowledge on a given subject. However, I strongly suggest that you do not try to bluff your way through such a conversation.

Why?

The person you are in dialogue with will easily discern if you "know what you are talking about". If you try to bluff him, then he could easily make you look stupid, which will disparage and belittle both you and the Company you are representing.

There is absolutely no harm at all in declaring your lack of knowledge on a subject.

There have been many times when I have been in the company of metallurgists who have blinded me both with their science and analyses. In these circumstances, I have asked just one question… Is the material fit for its intended purpose? That is all I wanted to know.

If you ask for the time, you don't really want to know how you make a watch!

Most people with specific knowledge or expertise on a subject relish the opportunity to show off their adroitness on the subject. Give them their "day in court". Rarely will they think the less of you. Indeed, there may be an advantage to you effusing such humility.

Between a Rock and a Hard Place

One Friday afternoon in Singapore, I received a call from a most honourable and trusted Far East customer. He wanted to borrow USD 30 million until the following Tuesday.

Most of our customers "maxed out" their traditional bank lines; thus, it was not unusual for situations to arise where we were asked to act as quasi-bankers. However, there were "situations" and "situations", and USD 30 million was an unusual amount.

Obtaining the funds was not the problem. We had the resources immediately available to us. The question was quantifying the risk and whether we should take the same.

The customer was prepared to sign all necessary documents and pledge all necessary guarantees. However, despite such preparedness, we were never going to have the security we needed physically in hand before the transfer of funds had to be effected.

So we faced the dilemma. Do we transfer the funds in the hope that the customer will repay us on time? Or do we tactfully decline his request?

If we adopted the latter course of action, whatever excuse we made, i.e. our bank forbade such a transfer, he would take such a reply as a slight against his character and trustworthiness. This would probably bring our business with him to an abrupt end. If we adopted the former course of action, we would have a sleepless weekend but, more importantly, run the risk of losing USD 30 million and having to face some uncomfortable questions from our bankers down the line.

We were between a rock and a hard place. I called my Chairman.

I have to explain at this juncture that our business with this client was worth over USD 30 million over a year.

We decided to lend him the funds. The transfer took place that afternoon. My loss of appetite promptly followed.

The weekend was a time of distraction and a contemplative time to assess the world come Tuesday evening when I would be seeking alternative employment!

Alas, on Tuesday, we received full reimbursement.

There are still valid arguments both for and against the decision we took. At the end of the day, you evaluate the risk against the future potential business.

Loss of Employment / Redundancy

Although I have briefly mentioned this subject matter above, I was in two minds as to whether to include this as a subject matter in this "book". By definition, it is a negative topic of conversation, but it is a situation which may, unfortunately, befall you. I hope it doesn't, but should you lose your employment, then my experience in this situation may help you both gain and retain some perspective on your life… at a time when your life looks dark.

I think the effects depend upon the time in your life when such an event happens.

I lost my employment on two occasions.

The first such experience occurred when I was in my 30s. I was working late one night just before Christmas, around 6.45 pm, when the Receivers entered our office and requested we immediately stop working. We were advised that our banks no longer supported us. We were tersely advised to go home but return tomorrow when further details would be announced. So, I left, but not without turning around once my shell-shocked feet had hit the pavement to see a chain and padlock being placed around the front door. What a state of affairs.

The next day we learnt that our aluminium and grain operations had dragged us all beneath the plimsol line. I was heading up the steel trading and, frankly, was making good money for the Company, so to be thrown to the wolves was just a little disconcerting!

When I was eventually "let go of", I think I must have been the only man walking down Piccadilly in an Aquascutum suit… out of a job!

Christmas that year was not great! My main concern was that I had two young children in private education, and I did not want to take them out of their schools.

I set about trying to pick up the pieces. This was easier when in my 30s than later in life (see below).

Today, I believe there is little stigma to losing one's employment. In the 1980s, there most definitely was. So, I had to maintain my self-esteem, re-invent myself and get the show on the road. I know I had a viable business.

First, I contacted my prime sources and customer-base to try to secure their continued support.

My second thought was how to establish reliable communication ....being dead without it. So, I made a pilgrimage to Boots, Croydon and purchased the best fax machine on the market (fax was the most modern form of electronic communication at the time) for the sum of GBP 1200.00…a king's ransom.

My first stroke of luck came when the manager of one of the properties which my previous company had been occupying contacted me, expressed sympathy for my plight and then advised me that the Receivers had not contacted him; thus, he assumed they were not even aware of his office. As he had received six months' rent up front, he would be delighted to help me out by permitting me to use the premises for free. This gesture had a marked effect on me. First, it helped me restore some self-respect by permitting me to don a suit and travel to work (a reflection on the automatism of my daily working life up to that time). Secondly, I had access to free communication. This was a major fillip as with no funds coming in, any help in covering the cost of communication was manna from heaven.

Every day I attended this place of work and went about trying to resurrect my career.

It was only after six weeks that the manager of the office advised me that the Receivers had located the office. A quick retreat was necessary with the compulsory covering of one's tracks. Our Volvo

Estate was immediately commandeered, driven with haste to London to scoop up my papers.

I now had to work from home. But, I still had to find finance if there was to be any viability to my venture… which was to carry on steel trading.

My meeting with a high-street bank lasted approximately 10 minutes. I retrieved my business plan from the manager of the bank when I realised he had either fallen into a comatose state or had resigned himself to using the revolver in the draw. Either way, high-street banks and start-ups are not a good cocktail.

Finance came by way of presenting businesses on a plate to other steel trading companies who generously permitted me to keep 50% of the profits.

I was eventually bought out after eighteen months.

The exposure to life without a secure income, and my primal instinct to preserve the entity of my family were sobering lessons in life.

I don't think you ever "get over" losing one's job. A chasm rises up before you. You have no security but a wealth of responsibilities. Your children continue to play in front of your eyes, totally unaware (or so you hope) of the machinations going through your head every second of the day. In time, and it can take a considerable amount of time, you learn to live with the upheaval and regain focus on the critical things in life… secure an income and keep your family together.

The second time I lost my employment, I was made redundant. I was in the latter stages of my working life… and it knocked me clean for six.

It happened when I was in Singapore. We were making good money for the Group, and since my arrival, I had established 11 new and profitable trade flows. Things were good. Then our banks discovered that our London office was using short-term finance for mid to long-term investments. Disastrous at the best of times. The banks wanted their money back, but London could not repay them. Fire sales ensued. Positions had to be liquidated, and a huge cost-cutting drive ensued. I, as Deputy M.D. for the Far East, was the second highest-paid employee in the Far East office. It took 20 seconds for me to be told my fate.

Throughout my working life, I created certain tenets in life which were my guiding principles, namely:

: **Work hard. You always need luck to succeed, but it won't come to you if you sit on your backside.

: **Be honest.

: **Be loyal.

: **The interests of the company are paramount. Think "Group".

The Group interests take precedence over the interests of, say, a subsidiary. To aspire to the Main Board, as previously mentioned, you need to first think like a Main Board member. If you don't, you will never achieve your goal.

: ** Look after your staff.

My redundancy knocked these values on the head. I was loyal and hard-working and made the Group a considerable amount of dosh.

When I was defending my position in those fateful minutes, I hit a wall of silence. Just silence. No one was interested in what I had achieved in the past years. So there we had it.

The days that followed were filled with anxiety and yet were vacuous. I was 62. I wanted to work till I was 70. I enjoyed my work, particularly the international travel and experiencing new markets and new cultures that presented themselves to me. Now....all gone.

Finding a new job at my age is never achieved by answering advertisements. It is only through contacts.

I was offered two jobs. The first was with a solid company which would, I believe, have provided me with the security I had recently craved for. But it was much the same as I had done for the last five years.

My brain went off tangent. Here was a safe, well-paid job which, in normal times, I would have immediately grasped, yet here I was, hesitating.

The buzz, the adrenaline rush, was created by the chase. Now that I had the offer in hand, I felt slightly deflated. In one sense, I had achieved a goal just by being offered the job. In addition, I was in receipt of an offer from another company, not so secure, but it opened up new opportunities and new experiences for me.

I took it! Yes, the risk was too enticing.

Who knows if I made the right decision. I did gain new experiences in the Middle East and parts of Africa I had not hitherto visited, so there were rewards, but there were also setbacks pertaining to honesty and integrity, which did not rest easy with me.

I was aware that there were people worse off than me… I had my health, or most of it, but frankly, not much else.

These were dark days.

There was only one cure for me.....work. But even my new career in the Middle East did little to quell my feelings that I had been badly let down by my past employers.

Pills are not the answer. Talking to "mates" may help more, but I really did not want to burden others with my predicament.

So, let me try to sum up the experience of loss of employment / redundancy and give you two thoughts to hang on to.

The first is that you never really get over the experience, but you do learn to live with it.

To be able to totally block the event from your mind is, I believe, just wishful thinking. I am not so sure you should even try, as it is just not realistic to do so. You have had a major shock. It's hard, very hard, but it is a fact of your life.

The dark days become fewer and the negative thoughts less intense, and whilst you may still harbour the shock and affront to your core values, you will learn to live with it.

The second point is that depending on your age and experience, you are probably more likely to find alternative employment through friends or contacts than by answering ads online or in newspapers or journals. I am not saying you go through your life developing relations for this sole purpose, but just bear it in mind as you forge friendships in your life.

Don't Discount Experience

Today we are in the throes of an advanced computer age. We live our lives through the prism of a screen.

What appears to be marginalised is the emotional intelligence or emotional quotient (EQ). This is the ability to assess, rationalise, and advise on any given situation. It defines an understanding of a situation and the ability to advise thereon.

To say there is a deficiency of EQ in young people is too strong an indictment, but such intelligence, by definition, is accumulated only over time, so it is perfectly understandable for young people to be found to be wanting here......to a point.

To help compensate, the younger generations should embrace the expertise and the experience that the older generations can offer. It's probably available at no cost. Why? Because you come to a time in your life when one wants to give back to society. Apart from the intrinsic value of such advice, it makes you feel wanted. It makes you feel good!

The problem today is that there is a stigma associated with age. The word "retirement" evokes pictures of dotage, a decline in mental alertness.

Watch out!

Whilst this image is not going to go away soon, we, in the fourth quartile of our lives, should look no further than ourselves to change society's attitude towards us.

I am embarking on a mentoring programme. It is early days, but the feedback from students has been very positive. Power!!

Aside from all the above exclamation marks, my message to the young is this… computer and digital awareness will take you far, but you will not be able to sustain that growth without EQ. Take a shortcut, talk to the guys in corduroy trousers… or ladies with the Launer handbags.

My Creed / Sense of Humour

What drives me? What is my belief? It's simple. I believe we all need luck in whatever endeavours we pursue. BUT........luck does not come to those sitting on their backsides. Work hard, work diligently, act with integrity, and you will then get the "breaks".

Stand up for yourself but always try to get others to work with you. This may exhaust your powers of persuasion, but it's worth being exhausted.

We are now close to the end of this book.

Let me add one more comment about how you should present yourself to the outside world and meet the challenges of everyday life. This involves, cultivating, nurturing one of the best, if not the best, weapon in your personal arsenal ....a sense of humour.

A sense of humour

: can break down any barrier. It is the most disarming non-weaponised missile at your disposal.

: reflects a self-confidence and the ability to see the positive side when facing a difficult or delicate predicament.

: is the most effective way to communicate your message.

: provides a stimulus in any given situation and helps maintain a sane perspective in life. It is a tonic for both the mind and body.

Try it. It works.

Last Word...Appreciation of Age...at My Age

So, this is my last thought. I hope I have given you some help in tackling a few of the challenges which you may face in your career.

I have a recurring problem with my heart. It's not broken, just subject to atrial fibrillation, which requires visits to my surgeon when the need arises.

So there I was, in his surgery, awaiting his summons. I lower myself into a couch, not quite knowing when gravity will determine when I experience the "hard landing". It comes unexpectedly. Now I thought, I knew the uncertainty Neil Armstrong felt moments before he landed on the moon. Like Mr Armstrong, I did wonder how I was going to extricate myself from the gravitational pull associated with a waiting room in Tunbridge Wells, this Sea of Tranquility. Is this the only place where you can both sit up and sit down at the same time?

In this time of reflection, I observed all those in the same waiting room. They were veterans. Warm faces. Sympathetic smiles. No doubt great and doting grandmothers, but age wrote its life across their faces.

But hold on......I am in surgery for people with heart problems. You are not going to get 30 or 40-year-olds in here... or hopefully not. We all have complaints which generally reflect one's age, so why the surprise!! Get over it, Mainwaring! I am in a generational time warp. I have sensible shoes, and the priority is to avoid slipping on pavements, not a catwalk. I have jerseys, which hopefully are fashionable but are primarily comfortable to wear, i.e. cover the mid-riff shadow. I have a cap which places me firmly in the gentry class, yet I live in a city.

Who am I trying to be? From where?

Good-bye.

Milton Keynes UK
Ingram Content Group UK Ltd.
UKHW050622150124
436051UK00009B/97

9 781962 840248